STRATEGY IN
JAPANESE
SWORDSMANSHIP

BOOKS BY NICKLAUS SUINO

The Art of Japanese Swordsmanship

Budo Mind and Body

Practice Drills for Japanese Swordsmanship

STRATEGY IN
JAPANESE
SWORDSMANSHIP

Nᴉᴄᴋʟᴀᴜs Sᴜɪɴᴏ

Wᴇᴀᴛʜᴇʀʜɪʟʟ
Boston & London
2007

Weatherhill
An imprint of Shambhala Publications, Inc.
Horticultural Hall
300 Massachusetts Avenue
Boston, Massachusetts 02115
www.shambhala.com

Martial arts techniques are dangerous if not practiced correctly. Neither
the author nor the publisher is responsible for your own choice to
practice these techniques; you do so at your own risk. Please use
caution when handling any weapons, and be sure to consult a qualified
teacher before attempting to perform any martial arts skills.

9 8 7 6 5 4 3 2 1

First Edition
Printed in the United States of America

⊗ This edition is printed on acid-free paper that meets the
American National Standards Institute z39.48 Standard.

Distributed in the United States by Random House, Inc.,
and in Canada by Random House of Canada Ltd.

Library of Congress Cataloging-in-Publication Data
Suino, Nicklaus.
Strategy in Japanese swordsmanship / Nicklaus Suino.—1st ed.
    p.   cm.—(Japanese swordsmanship)
Includes index.
ISBN: 978-1-59030-489-1 (pbk.: alk. paper)
1. Swordplay—Japan. 2. Iaido. I. Title.
GV1150.2.S86 2007
796.86—dc22
2007015543

To the 324 Gang:

Don, Greg, John, and Stevers

CONTENTS

ACKNOWLEDGMENTS

REFLECTING on all the support and encouragement I have had in martial arts is a humbling pastime. There have been so many people who have contributed that it sometimes seems I have played only the smallest part in my own career. To list everyone who has had an influence would be impossible, but there have been a few whose contributions are especially noteworthy.

Yamaguchi Katsuo, of the last great generation of Japanese swordsmen, died in January 2006 at the age of eighty-nine. He was a charismatic teacher who could astonish even *iaido* experts with his precise rendition of formal techniques. He was at his best in one-on-one training sessions, endlessly patient, technically exacting, and deeply interested in his art. One of the greatest kindnesses ever bestowed on me came in the form of the extra time he spent sharing the principles that underlie the techniques. Such explanations are a very rare thing in Japan. The usual approach is to teach the kata without much discussion. Yamaguchi Sensei advised me to think deeply about real interactions with swords. His explanations about how the techniques could be used to prevail in a match are the genesis of the approach taken in this book. Any errors, however, are my own.

My students, many of whom were accomplished martial artists before taking up iaido, have forced me to grow by constantly striving to improve themselves and their own students. Senseis Dan Holland and Nick Miller of ITAMA Dojo in East Lansing, Michigan, are seekers in the best sense of the word, always asking questions, always reading, always practicing, and always improving. Sensei Max Roach and his wonderful students at the Yama Oroshi Dojo in Salt Lake City have inspired me to share my most private ideas about technical and spiritual development in iaido. Sensei Frank Nieves of Iaido Miami has been very generous during my visits, encouraging his students to consider my technical suggestions despite his own fine credentials, and indulging my weakness for simple Cuban food. Sensei Andrew Bryant of the Indy Budokan, deeply interested in the history and development of iaido, has been a source of inspiration and support.

Three lovely women—Amy Prior, Carmina Lu, and Pamela Suino—sacrificed a great deal of time to pose with me in over nine hundred photos, many of which appear in this book. Beth Frankl, gracious and skilled martial arts editor at Shambhala, generously supported this project from its inception.

John Gage, Nihon jujitsu expert, training partner, and best friend of thirty years, has contributed in ways too numerous to count. My brother John Spears, having achieved ultimate success through intellect and sheer force of will, is now committed to the success of his friends. Jonpaul Rearick has transcended swordsmanship and become the most treasured of all possible friends, the number one fishing buddy. My wife, Pamela, endures my cranky intolerance yet still grows more generous and loving every day.

My heartfelt thanks to all these wonderful people—without you this book could not have been written.

STRATEGY IN
JAPANESE
SWORDSMANSHIP

INTRODUCTION

I N   M Y   F I R S T   B O O K , *The Art of Japanese Swordsmanship,* I provided instructions on the formal solo techniques of *Muso Jikiden Eishin-ryu Iaido.* The late Yamaguchi Katsuo, a tenth-degree *iaido meijin* (*meijin* means an acknowledged master) and extraordinary kendo expert, taught me these techniques in Tokyo. The purpose of *The Art of Japanese Swordsmanship* was to preserve and teach the formal checkpoints of swordsmanship, so it focused on technical matters more than either the strategic or internal aspects of swordsmanship. This is not to say that a diligent student could not learn strategy or improve his character by studying and practicing the formal techniques long enough. Indeed, as Miyamoto Musashi rightly stated, "The Way is in training." However, as a reference book, the specific purpose of *The Art of Japanese Swordsmanship* was to provide the foundation for kata (forms) training, rather than the theories of strategic swordsmanship.

In my second book, *Practice Drills for Japanese Swordsmanship,* I offered skill-building exercises for those who want to become experts with the sword. Some of these drills I encountered during my initial years of training in Japan. Others I created by dissecting formal *iaido* techniques in order to teach important concepts or skills. The purpose of *Practice Drills for Japanese Swordsmanship* was to help students develop the fitness and essential skills needed to become fluent in swordplay. Students who practice the drills may come to understand some strategic aspects of sword handling, but *Practice Drills for Japanese Swordsmanship* is not a strategy manual. Rather, it acts as a guide for those who want to improve their swordsmanship skills, whether those skills lie in the area of formal techniques or in practical application.

My third book, *Budo Mind and Body* (originally published as *Arts of Strength, Arts of Serenity*)—which is not just for swordspersons, but for martial artists of all stripes—addressed many internal aspects of training. In *Budo Mind and Body*, I tried to systematically explain useful practice methods, mindsets, and objectives for those martial artists who view their training as a way of life. I set out to help them become physically skilled, mentally acute, and, most important, aware of the spiritual aspects of their training. *Budo Mind and Body* is not a training manual, but a mentor in book form, designed to encourage, guide, and assist. Much to my delight, it has turned out to be a very popular book, but any instruction on strategy in the external sense of the word was implied in *Budo Mind and Body*, not explicit. Once again, it was left to the student to internalize the book's lessons and extrapolate fighting strategy from them.

This book, *Strategy in Japanese Swordsmanship*, takes the next step and directly discusses a tactical approach to training. It provides a framework for learning strategic swordsmanship, and it demonstrates techniques that help put the strategies into practice. The theme of this book is that, rather than passively absorbing the techniques of the sword, an ambitious student should establish in his or her mind the ultimate purpose of the art and work to master each technique in order to fulfill that purpose. To advance to the rarified level of master swordsperson, one must determine exactly what he or she wishes to accomplish in encounters with opponents. Everything a swordsperson does while training should move him or her closer to that goal. To again invoke the sword saint Musashi, in training one must "do nothing that has no purpose."

Even this book, however, is not an attempt at elucidating a grand theory of strategy that a swordsperson could use to triumph in all encounters with the sword. I have studied and practiced martial arts for forty years and have yet to discover such a theory. Instead, I have come to the conclusion that the ability to prevail in armed conflict is gained through careful consideration of technical issues, consistent practice, and ceaseless reflection. Mastery of strategic swordsmanship, like all great endeavors, is difficult. Therefore, in this book I offer some tools to help you become a great swordsperson: simple, practical skill-building drills and thought exercises to assist you on the path toward expert status. If you study these pages carefully and practice incessantly, constantly reflecting on how you can improve your ability and insight, you will find yourself a much more capable swordsperson. You should find that you have developed a heightened knowledge of your strengths and limitations, a keen awareness of detail, and an ability to sense the moods and intentions of those you face in the dojo. You may also find, as I have, that the practice of swordsmanship is one of the most rewarding activities you will ever encounter.

I

MAEGAKI (INTRODUCTORY MATTERS)

WHAT IS STRATEGY?

IN JAPANESE swordsmanship, our highest goal is expressed in the phrase *saya no uchi* or *saya no uchi no kachi,* which means "victory with the sword still in the scabbard." It is an exhortation to the swordsperson to recognize that physical combat is a last resort, and a reminder that a master strategist will find a way to win without fighting. Indeed, as Sun Tzu said, "To fight and conquer in all your battles is not supreme excellence; supreme excellence consists in breaking the enemy's resistance without fighting."

The road to such mastery is a long one, however. Before we can triumph with intellect or sheer willpower, we must have both a deep understanding of the principles of swordsmanship and a character that compels us to act in accordance with those principles. Such attributes are acquired through consistent, long-term practice, not only of the formal techniques, but also of practice drills and simple strategic development drills such as those presented in this book.

Strategy, as defined by the *American Heritage College Dictionary,* is "a plan of action . . . intended to accomplish a specific goal." The master swordsperson practices with two very specific goals in mind: (1) to cut the opponent while avoiding being cut, and (2) to move toward perfection of character. The first goal is external and theoretical, while the second is internal and, though esoteric, real. Both goals are critical to properly practicing our art, and every other goal or objective is derived from them. This book provides a plan of action intended to help you accomplish each of these two important objectives in your practice of Japanese swordsmanship.

Cutting an opponent while avoiding being cut is an external goal, focusing on our physical actions and those of our opponent. It is also a theoretical goal, because in our society we do not intentionally cut people. Since the Meiji Restoration, the Japanese sword has come to be considered life giving rather than life taking. (The Meiji Restoration was a series of political and cultural events starting around 1866 that led to enormous changes in Japan. With the reforms came much modernization and the adoption of Western technology. Swordsmanship, which came to be considered anachronistic, was transformed. Its practitioners de-emphasized its usefulness as a fighting art and instead began to focus on its benefits as a means of affecting character.) However, keeping the practical fighting purpose of our art in mind anchors our practice in martial realism and prevents it from becoming decadent. Every decision we make about how to hold a sword, how to stand, how to move, or how to think when facing an opponent, must be based on a principle found in sword fighting. To lose this grounding in martial reality would lead us to an art that would be little more than dancing or baton twirling with a sword.

Character perfection, on the other hand, is an internal goal, focusing on the condition of one's mind and spirit. It is also a real goal; though extraordinarily difficult, it is possible through practice to improve our discipline, our awareness, our integrity, and our ability to live harmoniously with universal principles. Moreover, while there is no need in modern times for us to actually fight with swords, there is a real need for us to refine ourselves and to seek betterment of the human condition. This is a worthwhile goal in any endeavor.

The wonderful paradox of swordsmanship is that the more diligently one pursues the first goal—learning how to cut an opponent while avoiding being cut—the more one progresses along the path toward the second goal—perfection of character.

This statement might surprise many people who do not understand the internal aspects of *budo* (martial arts). I have found it to be true, however. The more time one spends practicing kata, practice drills, and other swordsmanship training methods, the more the inner aspects fall into place. The converse principle is also true; the better one understands and harmonizes with one's rightful position in the world, the more effective one's swordsmanship becomes. Thus, the word "strategy" as used in this book applies both to the most effective way to wield a sword and the most effective way to ensure that one's swordsmanship is an exercise in spiritual forging. You should be content with nothing less.

TACTICS AND TECHNIQUES

To fully benefit from the lessons contained in this book, it is helpful to understand not only the meaning of the word *strategy*, but also the words *tactics* and *techniques*. The *Oxford English Dictionary* defines *tactic* as "a procedure or set of maneuvers engaged in to achieve an end, an aim, or a goal." Thus, while our strategy refers to our general plan of action, our tactics are the methods we use to accomplish the plan. These methods can be further broken down into techniques, such as the components of the tactics and drills presented in this book. These techniques are designed to instill in you the intuitive responses that will enable you to act tactically, efficiently accomplishing your strategic goals in each interaction with a sword.

Although strategy, tactics, and technique often overlap, being aware of the distinctions between them is useful in guiding our study. As an example, consider our reaction to the most basic attack—a straight downward strike with a sword. Our external goal in this encounter—our strategy—is, as always, to cut the opponent while avoiding being cut. There are many ways to accomplish this. A common tactic might be to move to the side, then counterstrike. One technique that might fulfill the requirements of this tactic would be to step forward and to the right with the right foot while raising your sword overhead, then pivot back and out of the way with the left foot while executing a beheading stroke.

Experienced practitioners will recognize this technique as part of the second half of the form called *Shato,* from the *Eishin-ryu Batto Ho no Bu* set.

As you can see, the strategy is accomplished through the tactics, which are comprised of the techniques. Being aware of the different aspects of each interaction allows us to focus our attention in such a way as to maximize the efficiency of our learning. Viewing an interaction broadly, we determine our goal. Narrowing our perspective, we decide on the best tactic or tactics to accomplish our goal. Finally, we select the techniques that comprise the tactics and practice them until our minds and bodies are completely comfortable with them. We then practice them even more, until we develop the reflexive ability and the knowledge we need to perform them at just the right moment. As you will see in the final section of this book, if we pursue our long-term practice with a properly introspective frame of mind, our training can affect our character in some very profound ways.

Always keep the overall strategy in mind when studying and practicing the techniques and tactics shown in this book. Repeat the drills over and over again, thinking about how they fit into the larger picture. Ask for feedback from your instructor, read as much as you can on the subject, watch training videos, or contact me to arrange a time when we can go over the techniques together. Most of the drills in this book appear very simple, but much of what is to be learned from them can only be understood after significant practice and consideration. There is much truth in the fighter's maxim stating that there are no advanced techniques, only advanced applications.

After each practice session, reverse your thinking process. Reflect on whether the techniques you chose properly fulfilled your tactical requirements and whether your tactics accomplished your goal in the best way possible. Every great martial artist I know has had a period of years of intense, even fanatical, training in which he obsessed about his art and practiced daily almost to the point of exhaustion. It should be no surprise to hear that the more diligently you pursue your craft, the better at it you will become. The art must become part of you, and you must eventually become part of the art. Treat your swordsmanship like the most important thing in the world, and you will be amazed at the positive changes you will experience. You will become a more effective, more efficient, more aware swordsperson and a more balanced, happier, more successful human being.

STATE OF MIND

Achieving the two essential goals of our practice in swordsmanship not only requires an acute awareness of the physical and mental aspects of each interaction, but an ability to feel the exchange of energy between the participants. Your state of mind during practice is crucial. A negative state of mind interferes with your ability to achieve each exercise's goal. Anger, impatience, and selfishness restrict your awareness and prevent you from discerning your training partner's intent.

Conversely, proper practice has a profound positive effect on your state of mind. Putting your body and mind into action by practicing these drills—if you are truly focusing on the key elements and asking yourself questions about your strategy—tends to displace anger, teaches patience, and demonstrates the virtues of cooperation. Happiness, patience, and cooperation facilitate the flow of energy between swordspersons and make it easier for each person to react properly. The more you are able to live in the moment, putting aside all extraneous thought and responding intuitively to the subtle shifts of advantage and disadvantage between you and your partner, the more you will be able to feel that energy. Getting to such a state is no easy task but, once you are truly aware of the energy component of swordsmanship, you can begin to learn to control your attacker's intent. You will be on your way to becoming a great swordsperson.

This is a most worthwhile task. It is no coincidence that the same qualities we cultivate in the dojo can help us become better people in general. Seekers after enlightenment try hard to develop certain qualities: to live in the moment, to put aside all extraneous thought, and to intuitively take correct action. When we study the carefully prescribed rules of advanced swordsmanship, we learn how to achieve these same desirable qualities. With time, practice, and a consistent effort to improve, we can also attain similar states of mind in our activities outside the dojo. Eventually, it is hoped, all our lives can be spent in a state of higher awareness. Getting to that point is what Japanese swordsmanship is all about.

2

SHODEN (FUNDAMENTAL CONCEPTS)

VISION

SECOND ONLY to the mind, a swordsperson's eyes are his most important tool. As a means of gathering information, they reveal much about our opponent: the position of her sword, the extension in her arms, the strength and mobility of her stance, and, to some extent, her intent. The eyes also allow us to express our own energy, and can therefore be used to deceive, neutralize, or dominate. By training our eyes, and our minds along with them, we refine our ability to gather information and express energy. Such training consists of focusing our eyes at the right place at the right time and focusing our minds on the right aspects of an interaction while doing so.

Broadly speaking, a swordsperson uses three levels of vision. The first level is the narrow focus used to study details when learning a new technique or concept. The second level is the middle focus used to watch our opponent's body to determine her distance, angles, and intent. The third level is a broad or big picture focus used to encompass the entire interaction without directing our attention to any particular location.

A more advanced version of this big picture focus involves not "looking" with the eyes at all, but "feeling" the opponent's intent. This is the ultimate way for a swordsperson to gather information, and it corresponds with the highest goals of our training. Being aware of an opponent's intent allows us to take evasive action just as an attack is conceived or, even better, to quash the opponent's intent before she is able to attack. Being able to adopt this state of mind at will is the result of years of intense study and requires a very keen awareness.

VISUAL ACUITY DRILLS

The following drills will help you learn how to move toward an advanced state of visual acuity. Train yourself to adopt the different focus levels at the appropriate time, including both the visual and mental aspects. The visual drills in this section involve directing your attention to a certain location while focusing the mind on a particular aspect of the interaction. Practice these drills using as many different skill development drills as you can. You can use them in all of the two-person drills in *Practice Drills for Japanese Swordsmanship,* as well as in any other legitimate *battojutsu* or *kenjutsu* drills you may know. Repeat each drill numerous times. Try to practice a little every day rather than for several hours only once a week. Repeated practice over many months, while you constantly strive to increase your visual acuity, will dramatically improve your ability to perceive strategic openings. We will begin with simple exercises. For safety, please use *bokuto* or *bokken* (wooden swords) for these and all the drills in this book unless otherwise noted.

Eyes on the Swords

Your goal in these exercises is to clearly discern the position of each sword and to understand how that position affects the balance of power in an interaction. To do so, you will engage your training partner and then use your eyes to glean as much information as possible about the swords' positions. Start by crossing swords with your partner. Focus your gaze directly on the point where the swords cross one another.

EXERCISE I: FOCUS ON THE SWORDS

Fig. 1. *The swords are crossed with no obvious advantage.*

Engage your mind in the transaction and take careful note of each of the following details:

- What is the angle of each sword edge?
- Are the edge angles identical?
- If not, which edge is more sharply angled?
- What is the overall angle of each blade?
- Are the blade angles identical?
- If not, which blade is more sharply angled?
- How "deep" is the crossing (how much of each sword extends past the crossing point)?
- Is one sword deeper than the other? If so, which one?

Without shifting your gaze, ask yourself what the answers to the questions above tell you.

For example, in the exercise that follows (see fig. 2), if one edge is angled more than the other, does that create an advantage for one swordsperson? What could the person with the advantage do to exploit that advantage?

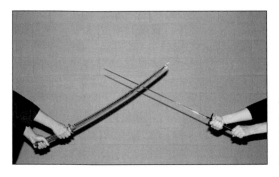

Fig. 2. The attacker (on the right) has angled the edge of her sword more than the defender has.

Your objective is to be able to immediately determine whether you are in a position of advantage or disadvantage, and what the appropriate response would be. If you are new to swordsmanship, some of the responses will be beyond you at this point, but you can develop your visual perception and your analytical ability by practicing each exercise. After you have read the other chapters in this book and developed a repertoire of swordsmanship skills, you will be able to determine appropriate tactical maneuvers and take action based on what you see and feel.

EXERCISE 3: ANGLE OF THE BLADE

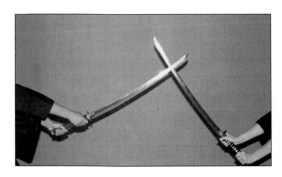

Fig. 3. The attacker (on the right) has angled the blade of her sword more sharply than the defender has.

If one blade is held at more of an angle than the other, does that create an advantage for one swordsperson? What could the person with the advantage do to exploit his advantage?

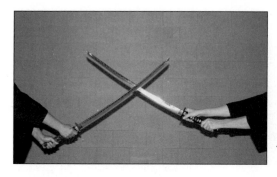

Fig. 4. The attacker (on the right) has extended her sword farther past the crossing than the defender has.

If one sword is deeper at the crossing, does that create an advantage for one of the swordspersons? What could the person with the advantage do to exploit his advantage?

Practice focusing your eyes on the swords, and then run through the questions in your mind. Do this over and over every day for a few weeks. You will soon find that your eyes naturally focus on the appropriate location and that your mind quickly finds the answers to the questions. If you continue to practice this and the other drills in this book, you will be able to immediately discern the weaknesses in the position of both swords (yours and your opponent's) and to act accordingly. Always keep the ultimate goals in mind.

Eyes on Your Opponent's Arms

Your goal in these exercises is to clearly discern the position of your opponent's arms and to understand how that position affects the balance of power in an interaction. To do so, you will engage your training partner and use your eyes to glean as much information as possible about her arm position.

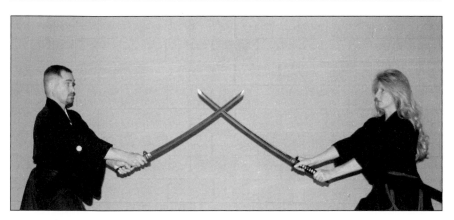

Fig. 5. The swords are crossed without an obvious advantage.

Cross swords with your training partner. Focus your gaze so that it encompasses your partner's sword, hands, and arms. This will be a slightly larger area of focus than you employed to study the positions of the swords.

Engage your mind in the transaction and take careful note of each of the following details:

- What sort of grip does your opponent have on her sword?
- Are your opponent's palms over the top of the sword handle?
- Are your opponent's hands far enough apart?
- What is the angle of your opponent's arms?
- What is the angle of your opponent's sword relative to her arms?

Ask yourself what the answers to the questions above tell you.

If your opponent's grip is weak, what weaknesses are inherent in the grip? What actions could you take to exploit her weak grip?

Fig. 6. The hands are placed too close together and the palms are not far enough over the top of the sword's handle.

In the illustration above, the opponent's hands are rotated too far to the sides of the sword handle. Note how this position decreases her ability to exert power through the blade. Consider the effects of such a grip. What can you do to avoid making the same mistake? How does her weakness affect the strategic balance in the interaction?

EXERCISE 7: ANGLE OF THE ARMS

Fig. 7. The attacker (on the right) has angled her arms too acutely.

Is the angle of your opponent's arms effective for extending power through her sword? If her arm angle is not effective, what actions could you take to exploit the weak angle?

Fig. 8. The attacker (on the right) has angled her sword too acutely.

Is the angle of your opponent's sword relative to her arms effective for extending power through the sword? If not, what actions could you take to exploit the weak angle?

Eyes on Your Opponent's Body

Your goal in the following exercises is to discern the position of your opponent's body and to understand how that position affects the balance of power in an interaction. To do so, you will engage your training partner and then use your eyes to glean as much information as possible about her body position.

Cross swords with your training partner (see fig. 9). Focus your gaze so that it encompasses your partner's arms, shoulders, hips, and knees. This will be a slightly larger area than you employed to see the swords or your partner's arms.

Fig. 9. The swords are crossed without an obvious advantage.

Engage your mind in the transaction and take careful note of each of the following details:

- What is the position of your opponent's shoulders?
- Are your opponent's shoulders squared? Raised? Asymmetrical?
- What is the position of your opponent's hips?
- Are your opponent's hips forward? Back? Neutral?
- What is the position of your opponent's forward knee?
- Is your opponent's knee bent? Straight?

Ask yourself what the answers to these questions tell you.

Fig. 10. The attacker (on the right) is holding her shoulders too high.

Is your opponent's shoulder position strong? If her shoulders are raised or asymmetrical, what weaknesses are inherent in that position? What actions could you take to exploit the weakness created by a faulty position?

Fig. 11. The attacker (on the right) has her hips too far back.

Is your opponent's hip position effective for maintaining balance? For extending power? If your opponent's hips are too far back, what weaknesses are created by that position? What actions could you take to exploit the weakness created by the faulty position?

Fig. 12. The attacker (on the right) has not bent her front knee sufficiently.

Is your opponent's knee position effective for maintaining balance? For moving quickly and with power? If her knee is not bent enough, what weaknesses are created by that position? If her knee is bent too much, what weaknesses are created by that position? What actions could you take to exploit the weakness created by the faulty position?

Eyes on Your Opponent's Eyes

Your goal in this exercise is to discern the attitude and intent in your opponent's eyes and to understand how those qualities affect the balance of power in an interaction. To do so, you will engage your training partner and then use your eyes to glean as much information as possible about her attitude and intent.

Cross swords with your training partner. Focus your gaze so that you look directly into his eyes (see fig. 13). This will be a very small area of focus. Some readers will find it difficult to look into another person's eyes while maintaining their composure. Practice this drill well and often, and you will find that you gradually become more comfortable performing techniques while maintaining eye contact.

Fig. 13. An attacker's eyes can reveal a great deal.

Avoid simply staring. Keep your mind engaged in an interaction and take careful note of each of the following details:

- Is your opponent looking directly back at you?
- Are his eyes wandering?
- Does his gaze appear strong and focused?
- Identify any weaknesses you can perceive in your opponent's gaze.
- Without shifting your gaze away from his eyes, identify any weaknesses you can detect in your opponent's sword, arm, or body position.

Ask yourself what the answers to these questions tell you. If your opponent is not looking directly back at you, where is he looking? If his eyes are wandering, what weaknesses might that indicate? Were you able to identify any weaknesses in his sword, arms, or body with information you gleaned from his eyes? What actions could you take to exploit the weakness you detected?

Continue to practice this drill with various partners. Try to increase the length of time you can maintain a focused gaze without blinking. It is crucial to prevent your mind from wandering during this drill. If you are simply staring in your partner's eyes while your mind wanders, you are teaching yourself bad habits. Instead, keep your mind occupied by analyzing your opponent's weaknesses and evaluating your own readiness for combat. Strengthening your gaze now will increase information flow dramatically when we start practicing moving drills.

Eyes on Details in Motion

The goal of these exercises is to discern the position of your opponent's sword, arms, and body during an interaction and to understand how those positions affect the balance of power in the interaction. To do so, engage your training partner in a moving drill and concentrate on using your eyes to glean as much information as possible about your opponent's position.

Perform the matching and advancing drills described below to cross swords with your training partner. (These and other drills are described in more detail in *Practice Drills for Japanese Swordsmanship.*) During each drill, focus your gaze on the appropriate area (crossing swords, or your opponent's arms, body, or eyes). Keep the previous questions about each area in mind so that you train yourself to immediately pick out weaknesses in your partner's techniques.

EXERCISE 14: MATCHING DRILL

Start by facing your partner, both of you in long stances (see fig. 14). (This stance is described in detail in the next chapter.) Your swords should be crossed with four to six inches of the tip of each sword extending past the other. For this drill, it does not matter which foot is forward in the long stance.

Both you and your partner step back to the intermediate position while raising your swords overhead (see fig. 15). You should now be on the ball of the foot that started as the forward or advanced foot, while the other foot is flat on the floor. Both knees should be bent, swords held overhead at a forty-five-degree downward angle, and elbows held wide.

Both you and your partner will step back into long stances while extending your swords to the ready position (see fig. 16).

Both you and your partner step forward to the intermediate position while raising your swords overhead (see fig. 17).

Fig. 14. Both partners are in long stances for the starting position in a matching drill.

Fig. 15. Both partners step back to the intermediate position while disengaging.

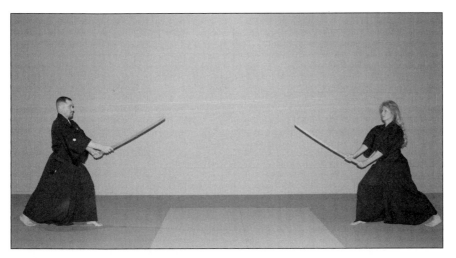

Fig. 16. Both partners step back into long stances in the ready position.

Fig. 17. Both partners step forward to the intermediate position while engaging.

Fig. 18. Both partners step forward into long stances resulting in a matched position to end the drill.

Finally, both you and your partner step forward to long stances while extending your swords to the crossed position.

Repeat this stepping pattern, engaging and disengaging, focusing on the swords or your opponent's arms, body, or eyes. Each time, select a level of focus and consciously run through the questions listed for that level. For example, at the moment of matching, focus on the point where the swords cross one another. Ask yourself whether one of the swords extends further beyond the crossing point than the other and whether this extension confers an advantage on you or your partner. Move slowly at first to give yourself time to run through the questions in your mind. Ask your partner to attack using various weak positions so that you can identify them. Gradually speed up as you become more comfortable with the drill and as the weaknesses and strengths of each position begin to seem obvious to you.

EXERCISE 15: ADVANCING DRILL

Choose one partner to be the attacker.

Run through the matching drill to the point of the first match: both you and your partner start in a matched position, step halfway back to the intermediate position, then back to a ready position. From the ready position, both you and your partner step forward to the intermediate position, then forward to the matched position.

Start the advancing drill from this matched position.

The attacking partner steps forward into the intermediate position, while the defending partner steps back to assume the intermediate position (see fig. 20).

The attacking partner steps forward to an extended sword position, while the defending partner steps backward to his own extended sword position, resulting in a match of swords (see fig. 21).

To disengage, the attacking partner steps back to the intermediate position, then to the ready position (see fig. 22).

Repeat this stepping pattern, engaging, disengaging, and switching attackers. Each time, select a level of visual focus and consciously run through the questions listed for that level. Have your partner deliberately adopt weak positions so that you can practice identifying them. Always ask yourself what each detail means and whether it confers a strategic advantage on you or your partner. Gradually speed up as you become more comfortable with the drill.

After practicing this and other drills many times, you should find that not only do the drills get easier but that you are noticing details more readily. Later, as we discuss the proper positions for your sword and your body, you should practice these drills again to deepen your ability to see the strategic aspects of each interaction.

Fig. 19. The matched position is the starting point for the advancing drill.

Fig. 20. The attacker (on the right) is advancing and the defender is retreating to the intermediate position.

Fig. 21. The attacker (on the right) has advanced and the defender has retreated.

Fig. 22. The attacker (on the right) has fully disengaged by returning to the
ready position.

THE BIG PICTURE

Highly focused levels of vision are extremely useful for swordsmanship training. They allow us to concentrate on a particular aspect of an
exercise and help us to swiftly recognize a point of weakness in our
opponent's position or attitude. Practicing the visual drills set forth in
the previous section also helps us train our minds to quickly adopt the
correct level of focus for a particular interaction.

For fast-paced practice, competition, or combat, however, too
much focus on a specific aspect of an interaction can lead to failure. A
swordsperson who is concentrating on the position of his opponent's
shoulders, for example, might fail to see the point of the sword as it
approaches his throat. A narrow view ignores what lies outside its
boundaries and thereby creates tactical weakness. Thus, to be truly
effective, the swordsperson must learn to cultivate a big picture view,
using a focused view only when the tactical situation requires it.

For training purposes, there are two different ways to practice the
big picture view. The first is with an analytical mindset, and the second
is with a reflecting mindset. In both, your eyes are open and directed
toward your opponent's eyes. Your gaze encompasses the entire interaction without focusing on any individual aspect. What differs between
the two methods is how you use your mind.

Analytical Mind—Static Drill

In practicing the analytical big picture view, you actively seek to determine your opponent's strengths and weaknesses. You can practice this in both static and active drills. In the static drill, you and your partner cross swords or, alternatively, face off in the ready position with several feet separating you, and do not move while each of you analyzes the other. You should practice this drill from both the close matched position and the more distant ready position.

As you practice this drill, it is crucial that you maintain the big picture view, not focusing on your partner's sword or any particular part of his body. Without moving your eyes, ask yourself the same sets of questions that you asked in the previous drills. What is the angle of your opponent's blade? Are your opponent's arms sufficiently extended? Is your opponent's stance strong? What are your opponent's weaknesses, and what could you do to exploit them? Repeat this drill with different opponents until you can quickly detect variations and identify the openings they create. As you improve, you will be amazed at how much you can determine about your opponent simply by observing him standing in front of you.

Analytical Mind—Moving Drill

In the moving version of the analytical big picture drill, go through the matching and advancing drills set forth in the previous section. As you practice, continue to maintain a strong gaze in the direction of your opponent's eyes, but do not focus specifically on them. Instead, try to observe the entire interaction, and analyze the positional strengths and weaknesses.

A word of warning is necessary here. Properly performing the drills in this section requires an adept practitioner. Use caution, since you may not anticipate dangerous situations while your mind struggles to maintain the proper focus. Start out slowly, agree in advance with your training partner that you will watch out for one another's well-being, and avoid speeding up until you are comfortable with each drill. For most students, truly developing comfort in these exercises will require repeated practice sessions spread out over a period of months. Don't give up if it takes some time. Instead, continue working through the drills in later chapters and keep coming back to these drills as you progress. Eventually, your mind will open up and you will be able to adopt the correct visual attitude without effort.

Reflective Mind—Static Drill

In the reflective big picture view, your mind is fully engaged in the interaction, but you do not focus on any particular aspect of your opponent's sword, stance, or motions. Your eyes and your mind act as mirrors, simply reflecting your opponent's actions without stopping on any one aspect. This is the beginning of the advanced state of mind that involves sensing an opponent's intent. At this stage, however, it is important to use your eyes as a source of information and to stay intent upon seeing, rather than feeling, the strategic aspects of an interaction.

Cross swords with your partner. Look toward your partner's eyes, keeping your own gaze energetic, but don't focus on any particular part of your partner's body. Keep your mind open, breathing deeply. Maintain the position and eye contact as long as you can keep your mind from focusing on any single aspect of your opponent.

If your mind centers on a detail or begins wandering, immediately break eye contact and move out of the matched position. Pause a moment, then cross swords again and let your partner attempt the drill. Alternate partners and repeat the drill numerous times in each practice session. Over time, you will be able to maintain the reflective mind for longer and longer periods. However, be careful to distinguish between the reflective swordsperson's state of mind and a simple trance or blank state of mind. The swordsperson's mind is always energetic and engaged in an interaction, and thus it is ready to respond instantly to any change in the balance of power. A person who simply stares while letting her mind go slack will be unable to respond quickly when the need arises.

There is no need to maintain this state of mind for any great length of time while standing still. If you find that you are able to maintain the correct state of mind through five or six deep breaths, you should attempt the moving part of this exercise.

Reflective Mind—Moving Drill

Perform the matching and advancing drills set forth in the previous section. This time, as you practice, continue to maintain a strong gaze in the direction of your opponent's eyes, but do not focus on them. Do not try to analyze any positional strengths and weaknesses. Instead, let your consciousness reflect the whole interaction as though it were a mirror.

Start out slowly, agreeing in advance which partner is performing the mental aspects of the drill so the other partner can monitor the exercise for safety. Practice the drills until you can perform them smoothly without getting distracted by technical details. Keep coming back to them as you learn more about the other aspects of swordsmanship. Be thoughtful, constantly reflecting on the progress you make in practice, striving to move closer to your goals. Be patient; these skills are advanced and take time to develop. Be active, always forcing yourself to move more deeply into the purpose of each exercise and never allowing yourself to be complacent.

The reflective big picture mindset in swordsmanship is ultimately the same as the "no mind" state sought by Zen practitioners. In such a state, our consciousness reflects the events around us without appraisal or judgment. This allows our trained responses to occur immediately, without interference by our evaluative or logical minds. If the system of responses and attacks we have studied is a sound one, then our reactions will be both correct and instantaneous. In the limited world of the dojo, we can approach perfection by diligently training then adopting the reflective big picture mindset when sparring. In life outside the dojo, the challenge is much greater because of the infinite variety of situations we encounter. It is possible, however, to make significant progress toward right action by applying the lessons learned in the dojo.

SWORD HANDLING

The sword provides the means both to cut an opponent and to block an opponent's attacks, fulfilling our first goal in swordsmanship training—to cut an opponent and avoid being cut. Like our eyes, the sword is a means of gathering information. When our sword contacts our opponent's sword, we can feel her strength or weakness and the direction of her potential attacks. We can also use our sword to express energy and, ultimately, to deceive, neutralize, or dominate our opponents. By engaging our minds and learning to wield the sword properly, we improve our ability to analyze information about an opponent's tactical moves. By constantly striving to become better swordspersons, to increase our ability to transmit and receive information and energy through our swords, we engage our entire personalities in the business of swordsmanship. Eventually, if this is done in the proper spirit of realism (ensuring that all our motions have a specific martial purpose), our character will be affected in a very positive way.

To truly become an expert swordsperson, you must train with your sword until it becomes part of you. When an advanced swordsperson takes up a sword in her hands, she immediately senses the location and position of the edge, the tip, the back of the blade, and the butt of the handle. You, too, should be able to feel the directions in which you can move your sword strongly and those directions in which it would be weak to move. You should be aware of your strategic strong points, your opponent's strengths, and the positions from which you might be vulnerable to an attack. At your best moments, your sword should almost vibrate with energy—an energy that can be transmitted to your opponent, whether for good or ill.

Needless to say, it is not easy to come by this ability. It requires a good education in sword handling, consistent practice, and endless reflection on your own strengths and weaknesses, whether physical, mental, or spiritual. Most swordsmanship students vastly underestimate the practice time and the degree of mental focus required to master this art. Practice the drills over and over again, always with an inquisitive mind, always seeking to understand the relationship between position and strategic advantage, always striving to sense more deeply the exchange of energy, and always recognizing that a swordsperson's well of awareness has no bottom.

All the drills in this chapter are relatively simple, but this simplicity is deceptive. Expertise in swordsmanship does not lie in complexity, but in a deep intuitive understanding of the most basic aspects of swordplay, including the position of the swords, distancing, timing, angles, and the energy of your opponent. In time, the drills will come to represent something more than mere exercises in positioning the sword. Where the beginning student perceives only her opponent and her sword, you will understand whether your opponent is far enough from you, whether your opponent's sword is wielded strongly or weakly, whether it occupies an effective strategic space, and whether his energy is active or passive.

My teacher, Yamaguchi Katsuo, said: "The sword is like the mind, and if the sword is upright, the mind is upright. But if the mind is not upright, the sword can never be wielded properly." This neatly summarizes the difference between swordspersons at different skill levels. It is truly a participant's character that determines whether he is a poor, fair, good, or great swordsperson.

SWORD-HANDLING DRILLS

Grasping a Sword

Before we begin our discussion of how to grasp the *katana,* the Japanese sword, a word about the swords themselves is in order. As I explained in *The Art of Japanese Swordsmanship,* the *katana's* unique shape requires that it be used in a specific manner. The classic *katana* has a relatively short handle (often less than ten inches) and a relatively long blade of approximately thirty inches. The relationship of the sword's two sections is a good indication that our cuts are not meant to be accomplished using leverage. If they were, the handle would be much longer in relation to the blade.

In the past decade, many swords have appeared in the North American market with handles well over twelve inches in length. I have read explanations for this construction suggesting that the longer handle was added to increase a swordsperson's leverage in order to make stronger cuts or to be able to place their hands further apart, facilitating a more dramatic differential between their hands' movement during a cut. However, I have only heard these explanations in North America. When I lived in Japan, I met dozens of high-ranking swordspersons and many well-known teachers with confirmed historical lineages in traditional iaido. None of these people ever encouraged me to use leverage in cuts, and no respected teacher has ever advised me to think of the katana as a leverage tool. Nor did I ever see a swordsperson with legitimate credentials wielding a *katana* with a handle much longer than ten or eleven inches.

The sword is not used to chop or hack, as it would be if a person's two hands were placed farther apart. A *katana*'s blade is not bulky enough to survive the stress of being used like an axe, and nothing else about its design suggests that it should be so used. It is an elegant slicing tool designed to be used in a specific manner. The sword is grasped and swung for cutting in a precise and clearly defined way. For more detailed information on how to grasp and wield a sword for iaido, please take a look at my other books on this subject, *The Art of Japanese Swordsmanship* and *Practice Drills for Japanese Swordsmanship*. For the purposes of this book, however, we need only a broad understanding of the right and wrong ways to handle a sword, and how our handling of it affects the balance of power in an interaction with another swordsperson.

You hold a sword in both hands, edge down, with your right hand forward and your left hand back. The first knuckle of your right index finger should be touching the *tsuba* (sword guard). Your left hand should be as far back on the handle as it will go while keeping all your fingers on the handle. Most of the strength in your grip comes from the little finger and the ring finger, so it is important for them to remain on the handle. Your grip should be firm, but not tight, and your hands should not be tense. Your wrists should be rotated inward so that your palms are over the top of the handle. This rotation facilitates two of the most important goals in grasping the sword: the ability to direct power through the edge and the ability to control the blade at the end of the cut.

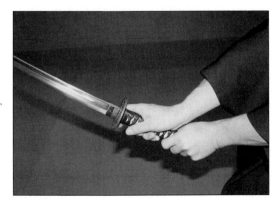

Fig. 23. The correct way to grip a katana *is with the wrists rotated inward.*

Fig. 24. The grip is incorrect—the palms are rotated too far outward.

Don't let your hands rotate outward during cuts; this will allow your palms to move toward the sides of the handle, which will create weakness in both cutting power and control. You cannot direct power through the edge well when your palms are on the side or at the bottom of the handle, nor can you control the wobbling of the blade during a cut.

Testing Your Grip

Your goal in these drills is to cultivate the correct, strong grip, using three of the many positions in which it is necessary to direct power through the blade. Recognize that your practice will require many other positions, and take the time to cultivate a strong grip that can be applied in each one. The key during these grip drills is to concentrate on the position of your hands, wrists, and palms, and to gain an understanding of how their position affects your ability to direct power through the sword.

EXERCISE 16: STRENGTHENING YOUR GRIP

Grasp your sword in both hands, keeping your palms over the top of the handle (see fig. 25). Point the sword at the throat of an imaginary opponent. This is called the extended ready position. Have your partner push upward on the midpoint of the blade while you hold your sword in the extended ready position, first with just your right hand, then with just your left hand, and finally with both hands. Try to extend strength through your arms, wrists, and palms so that you can

Fig. 25. The sword is held in the extended ready position while a training partner pushes upward.

resist the push without tensing your muscles. Repeat this drill regularly to improve your understanding and to build strength in your wrist and arm muscles.

EXERCISE 17: EXTENDING POWER THROUGH THE GRIP

Your grip should also be tested in the extended ready position and in the finish position for a high strike. In both these positions, your hands are oriented much like in a major downward cut. However, in the high strike position (*ganmenate*), your hands are rotated inward to ensure that your palms are over the top of the handle, but your arms are extended further away from your body and your wrists are cocked slightly forward (see fig. 26). These changes help to align your blade so that you can extend power forward. When testing for strength in this position, your partner should check to see that you can direct power to a point about six inches back from the *kissaki* (sword tip).

Fig. 26. The sword is held in the high strike position while a training partner pushes it upward at a point six inches back from the tip.

EXERCISE 18: EXTENDING POWER IN THE HIGH STRIKE POSITION

Once again, for the high strike position, extend your arms further and cock your wrists forward. It can be helpful to have a partner stand in front of you so you can practice touching her forehead with the tip of your sword. When testing for strength, your partner should grasp the tip of your sword and press back toward your hands (see fig. 27).

Positioning the Sword

Just as we saw with the grip, a cut or parry with a sword is much stronger when done in accordance with certain checkpoints. These checkpoints will vary depending on the exact action you are trying to complete, but in each one, there is a "sweet spot," or ideal range within which the most power can be directed through your blade. Being able to generate this power is critical for strong cuts and blocks. In this section, we will consider three techniques: *nukitsuke* (the classic iaido horizontal draw and cut), the forty-five-degree downward draw and cut, and the extended ready position. Each technique shares four key as-

Fig. 27. The sword is held in the high strike position while a training partner pushes it back toward the hands.

pects: full extension in the arm or arms, a strong arm angle relative to the body, a strong wrist position, and a strong sword angle.

EXERCISE 19: HORIZONTAL DRAW AND CUT

In *nukitsuke,* you draw your sword and then cut on a horizontal line at about the height of your opponent's throat. The proper sequence in an actual draw would involve drawing your sword until it cleared the scabbard, closing your grip to achieve a strong wrist position and blade angle, and moving your right arm to the right so that your sword cuts across in a clean, powerful, horizontal line. In this exercise, we will vary the order of the motions to show how power is directed from your body, through your arm, and into progressively more extended parts of your blade.

Your right arm is the first element to isolate in a horizontal draw. Start in a long stance with your back leg locked and your front knee bent. Draw your sword with the butt of the handle pointing at your partner's throat, continuing until your right arm is completely straight. Be sure your elbow is locked. Control the tip of your sword by gently squeezing it with the thumb and forefinger of your left hand. Have your partner check your strength by pressing against your right hand, directly back toward your body (see fig. 28). You should feel a line of strength originating where your back foot contacts the ground and extending up through your left leg, hips, torso, and right arm to your hand.

Besides establishing linear strength by fully extending your right arm, during the cutting portion of this motion it is also necessary to generate horizontal strength with your right arm. As in the previous test, draw your sword with the butt of the handle pointing at your partner's throat, continuing until your right arm is completely extended without actually drawing. Have your partner check the strength of your cutting motion by placing her hand on the outside of your right wrist and pushing horizontally to your left while you resist (see fig. 29). Focus your awareness on your shoulder and chest muscles, paying close attention to how hard you have to work to maintain your position. Experiment by testing your right arm's strength in various angles. A more acute angle relative to your body will be weaker, and a more obtuse angle will be stronger.

In *Eishin-ryu Iaido,* we stop the horizontal draw and cut when our arm is at a forty-five-degree angle relative to our shoulders. This is generally accepted as the farthest position along the horizontal arc in which

Fig. 28. After the right arm is completely straight, the training partner checks for linear strength.

Fig. 29. As the sword is drawn, the training partner pushes the right hand horizontally to the left.

an arm can generate strength. In some other forms of iaido, the draw is carried through until the swordsperson's arm is at a ninety-degree angle to increase the length of her slicing motion. Whatever ending position you choose, be sure you understand the range through which your *nukitsuke* is strongest. Practice sufficiently so that your draw moves into this range at the exact time your cut would make contact with an opponent's body.

Once you understand how to use your arm to generate strength in the *nukitsuke*, you must extend that strength through your blade. Your wrist is the link between your arm and your blade. In order to achieve a strong wrist position for the cutting portion of the *nukitsuke*, close your hand firmly over the handle as your blade leaves the scabbard. This brings your wrist to a square position, with the bones of your hand in line with the bones of your arm. You then cock your wrist slightly toward your little finger to drive power through your blade.

To test the power in your wrist, have your partner push horizontally against the blade toward your left shoulder (see fig. 30). At first, your partner should push against the third of the blade that is closest to your hand. As you get better and stronger, your partner can push farther out on the blade where the leverage exerted against your wrist is greater. Experiment with different wrist positions while keeping your

Fig. 30. When the sword is drawn, the training partner pushes horizontally against the blade to the left.

arm fully extended. Keep your overall arm angle within its range of strength. Once your wrist is cocked at its strongest angle, you will be able to exert significantly greater power through your sword. This is the angle you want to achieve before or just as the sword makes contact with your opponent's body.

If you have successfully completed all three aspects of this exercise, the angle of your sword relative to your arm and body should be correct. The blade should be oriented so you can direct the maximum amount of power through your target. The next step is to consider your sword's position relative to your opponent's body (for a cutting draw) and to the angle of your draw (for a deflection or parry).

More will be said about angles and distancing in a later chapter, but for now you should make sure that your sword contacts your opponent and moves horizontally, passing from one side of her body to the other. If you contact your opponent's body with your sword at a weak angle or fail to make contact at all, your *nukitsuke* will not achieve its desired purpose. Keeping in mind that this motion is not designed to cut a body in half, but merely to slice the throat or chest, practice this drill repeatedly with your partner (carefully, to avoid injury!). Make your initial contact with a strong sword position and follow through so that the finished position is beyond your partner's body (see fig. 31).

Fig. 31. The attacker's sword (on the left) should make contact with the defender's body at a strong angle.

For a deflection or parry, your sword should make contact with your opponent's arm just before she completes her draw (see fig. 32). As before, your own sword angle should be strong just as contact is made, and you should have the intent to follow through to a finished position beyond your opponent's body. This motion is designed to cut your opponent's right arm, making it impossible for her to complete the draw, thereby protecting you from being cut.

Fig. 32. The attacker's sword (on the left) should make contact with the defender's arm just before she is able to draw.

Many systems of iaido employ a draw that begins with the handle of the sword being drawn high and to the left until the sword is free of the scabbard, and ends with a forty-five-degree downward cut or parry, to the opponent's right clavicle or right wrist as she grasps her sword. *Eishin-ryu* practitioners will recognize this draw as the opening move from *Tsuigekito* from the *Batto Ho no Bu*. It also appears in the *Shiho Giri* form in the All Japan Iaido Federation's *Toho* set and in several other forms. It is another excellent technique for studying the four components of extension (full extension in the arm or arms, a strong arm angle relative to the body, a strong wrist position, and a strong sword angle).

Start in a long stance with your left leg back and your right knee forward. Draw upward and toward your opponent's right shoulder, continuing until your right arm is straight and your elbow is locked. Control the tip of your sword by squeezing it with the thumb and forefinger of your left hand. As you did in the last drill, have your partner test your arm's linear strength by pushing your hand directly back toward your body (see fig. 33). You should be able to extend power in this position from your left foot through to your right hand. The linear strength of your fully extended right arm is a prerequisite to creating strength for a cut.

From the point at which your right arm is fully extended, release the tip of your sword and move your right arm at a forty-five-degree angle downward and to the left. Stop at various points in this arc, and have your partner press against the outside of your wrist, directly opposing the path of your downward motion (see fig. 34). Be aware of your shoulder and chest muscles. Determine where the motion feels strongest and where it feels weakest. Your goal is to make contact with the target just as your arm reaches its strongest position.

Your strength must now be transmitted to your blade. Starting with your arm fully extended and your left hand controlling the tip of your sword, release the tip and close your hand firmly over the handle. Bring your wrist to a square position so your sword is at a right angle to your arm. To test the power in your wrist, have your partner push

Fig. 33. While the sword is drawn upward toward the defender's right shoulder, he pushes against the drawing hand.

Fig. 34. While the arm is moved downward at a forty-five-degree angle, the training partner pushes against the right wrist.

Fig. 35. After the sword is drawn and moved to a right angle relative to the right arm, the training partner pushes against the blade.

against your blade at the forty-five-degree downward line of your cut (see fig. 35).

Your partner should initially push against the third of the *bokken* that is closest to your hand, and then later farther out on the blade to increase the leverage. Move your arm and sword through the entire range of the cut and test your strength at various points. Keep in mind that this cut has an important slicing component, which means that some of its effectiveness comes from your arm's downward motion rather than from the blade's outward motion. Because of the slicing effect, there is a range of acceptable points at which you can make contact with your opponent's wrist or body. Nevertheless, you should ensure that you are in a strong position at the point of contact and can maintain strength through the end of your cut.

Now consider your sword's position relative to your opponent's body. If you are planning to make a cut or parry to the wrist, practice following through with this drawing motion until you make contact (see fig. 36).

To cut your opponent at the clavicle, modify your aim to strike there. For either target—the wrist or the clavicle—carefully touch your partner with the edge of the *bokken*. Follow through with a slicing motion by continuing to move your right arm down on a forty-five-degree

Fig. 36. The attacker's sword (on the right) should make contact with the defender's wrist at the strongest point along the attacker's forty-five-degree downward arc.

Fig. 37. The attacker's sword (on the right) should contact the defender's clavicle at the strongest point along the attacker's forty-five-degree downward arc.

line (see fig. 37). Repeat this drill until the correct distancing and strength in your cut become reflexive.

EXERCISE 21: EXTENDED READY POSITION

The extended ready position is rarely found in iaido forms, more often being used in *kenjutsu*, *battojutsu*, and aikido. It serves as a means of establishing a defensive distance, sets up thrusting and slicing attacks, and allows you to establish contact with your opponent's sword. With contact comes the ability to feel the motions of the other person's sword, allowing for an exchange of energy. This makes it possible to defend against attacks and to read your opponent's intent. Just as with the two draws that we have already considered, the extended ready position requires strong arms, a strong arm angle and wrist position, and a strong sword angle.

Start in an upright stance with your left foot back. Grasp your sword in both hands and point the tip at your partner's throat. Fully extend both arms with your palms over the top of the handle. This allows you to transmit strength from your arms into your blade. Have your partner check the extension of your arms by pushing against your fists, toward your shoulders (see fig. 38). The proper arm position is a forty-five-degree angle relative to your body. Though it is difficult to test the strength of this angle without taking into account the position of your sword, have your partner push downward against the top of your hands. Experiment by holding your arms higher and lower than forty-five degrees until you find the position that feels strongest.

The proper position for your sword is a 135-degree angle relative to your arms. Your arms are fully extended and held at the requisite forty-five-degree angle, with your palms over the top of the handle. You can adjust your wrists to bring your sword to the correct angle. Once achieved, this angle will create strength against resistance from either the top or the bottom. Your partner can help you test this strength by pushing against the middle of your blade (see fig. 39). As always, experiment by increasing and decreasing the angle in your wrists. As you get better at extending strength though your sword, your partner can test your position by pushing near the tip of the blade.

Fig. 38. The attacker holds her sword in the extended ready position, and her partner checks her strength by pushing against the top of her hands.

Fig. 39. The attacker holds her sword in the extended ready position, and her training partner pushes upward against the middle of the sword to check her strength.

Cultivating "Feel" in a Blade

Once you have developed an understanding of how to grasp the sword and how to position it for maximum strength, you can begin to cultivate "feeling" in the blade. This is the next step in the process of making your sword a virtual extension of your arms and hands. The goal is to move your sword and make contact with your opponent's sword and body while simultaneously concentrating on the tactile feedback that runs through your blade and into your hands. It also involves learning to move in such a way as to gain both maximum feel and strategic advantage.

These tactile drills help to develop a sense of distance, improve timing, and cultivate a deep intuitive understanding of how to transmit strength through your body and arms. For all of these drills, start with both yourself and your partner in the extended ready position, swords crossed, and the end of your sword in contact with the right side of your partner's sword.

EXERCISE 22: EXTENDING

Being careful to maintain contact between the weapons, extend forward with your arms and body until the tip of your sword touches

Fig. 40. The attacker (on the left) extends forward with his arms and body until the tip of his sword touches the defender's body.

your partner's body. Be sure to cover as much of the distance as possible by extending your arms and as little as possible by leaning forward. After touching your partner, return to the extended ready position, maintaining contact between your swords the entire time. As soon as you return to the extended ready position, your partner will extend forward to touch you.

There is no need to perform this drill quickly. Though it seems simple, it actually provides a great deal of feedback. It will help you develop a sense of where your sword blade is and how strong it is relative to your partner's. Concentrate on the sensation of the swords sliding against each other, the feeling of extension when you contact your partner's body, your sense of distance from your partner, and how safe or exposed you feel at each point in the extension. Once you are comfortable with this drill, repeat it with your eyes closed.

EXERCISE 23: DEFLECTING

With both you and your partner in the extended ready position, have your partner extend forward, as in the extension drill, trying to touch your chest with the tip of her sword. Just as your opponent's motion begins, turn your edge inward, keeping your arms fully extended, to deflect her attack. You can accomplish this with a slight turn of your

Fig. 41. While the attacker (on the right) extends, the defender deflects with a slight turn of his wrists and shoulders.

wrists and shoulders. Try to make the deflection as small as possible, just large enough to ensure that the attack passes harmlessly by. The tip of your sword should be extended so that it touches the center of your partner's abdomen just as she reaches full extension. Be sure to maintain contact with your opponent's sword throughout.

After reaching full extension, your attacker will return to the extended ready position. You will attack next, and the drill can continue back and forth. The two swords should always stay in contact with one another. Concentrate on the areas listed for the extension drill—the sensation of the swords when they connect, your sense of distance from your partner, and how safe or exposed you feel—and also on the exact angle and the arm strength required to deflect and counter. Once you are comfortable with this drill, repeat it with your eyes closed.

EXERCISE 24: BLOCKING HIGH

Both you and your partner start in the extended ready position. Your partner will extend forward and up, trying to touch your face with the tip of her sword. While maintaining extension in your arms, and without losing contact between the two swords, lift the handle of your

Fig. 42. While the attacker attacks high, the defender blocks.

sword toward your upper left, blocking the attack with the middle of your blade. Once the attack is blocked, have your partner test your strength by pushing down on your blade with hers. Your partner will then withdraw by returning to the extended ready position. As she does so, extend your sword until you also resume the extended ready position. Avoid breaking contact between the blades. You can then attack high while your partner blocks, and continue alternating in the role of attacker.

Pay special attention to maintaining contact and to the feeling of relative safety or danger at each point during this drill. Be careful when you move from the high block back to the extended ready position because you may experience defensive weaknesses the first few times. Always look for openings in which you could break contact, deflect, or attack. Once you are comfortable with this drill, repeat it with your eyes closed.

EXERCISE 25: PRESSING DOWN

Both you and your partner start in the extended ready position. Your opponent extends forward, trying to touch your abdomen with her sword. While maintaining extension in your arms, and without breaking sword

Fig. 43. When the attacker (on the right) extends forward, the defender presses down to deflect.

contact, press downward on the top of your opponent's sword as it slides forward, deflecting it downward and to your left. Turn your shoulders slightly—right shoulder forward and left back—to help redirect the attack to your left side.

Once the redirection is complete, your attacker will withdraw, returning to the extended ready position, and you will attack. The drill goes back and forth, both you and your partner maintaining contact between swords at all times, with one extending and one pressing down each time. Once you are comfortable with this drill, repeat it with your eyes closed.

EXERCISE 26: BREAKING CONTACT

Though this chapter is devoted to developing strength and a feel for your blade, as opposed to actual fighting drills, a brief look at what happens when contact is broken may be helpful. The goal is to help you experience the strategic difference between a situation in which there is contact between swords and one in which contact is broken.

Face your partner in an upright stance, both partners having the left leg back. Cross swords in the extended ready position. Your part-

Fig. 44. When the attacker (on the right) breaks contact, the defender extends straight in.

ner will then move her sword to her right, breaking contact. At that moment, extend forward with your arms and body to gently touch your partner's chest with the tip of your sword. Be sure that your partner moves her sword far enough to the right that it does not hit or impale you!

After touching your partner's body with your sword, return to the extended ready position. Your partner will do the same. Repeat the drill with the roles reversed, always paying careful attention to the feeling in your sword, hands, and arms at the moment that contact is broken. You can also practice the high and low attacking drills presented in this section with one partner deliberately breaking contact. Study how the break provides an opportunity for an alert swordsperson to take the center position. When you are comfortable with these drills, practice them with your eyes closed and repeat them many times.

EXERCISE 27: COMBINING DRILLS

After you and your partner are comfortable with each of the drills in this section, begin to combine them. Start very slowly for safety. Have your partner attack straight in, high, or low, or break contact, in random order. For each type of attack, you should respond correctly, either maintaining contact or taking over the center. As both you and your partner become more comfortable with the drills, you can trade back and forth, add speed and variations, and, eventually, practice with your eyes closed. At all times, be careful not to injure your partner. Focus your attention on the feeling in your blade, hands, and arms. In time, the blade will come to feel like an extension of your arms, and you will be able to determine a great deal about your partner's actions even with your eyes closed.

When both you and your partner are comfortable combining the drills, you can practice them without any particular formality, stepping in various directions and attacking in any reasonable manner. Eventually, the drill will take on the character of *randori,* or freestyle practice. You and your partner may speed up, adding realism to the attacks, always being careful not to hurt one another, of course. If you are using *bokken* and limiting the amount of force you use, you should be able to practice this drill for hours without any injury more serious than a bruised finger or two. After many months of practice, you will feel the free flow of energy from one participant to the other, and you will find that you can readily control that energy. This is the point at which real strategic swordsmanship begins.

3

CHUDEN
(INTERMEDIATE
CONCEPTS)

DISTANCING

DISTANCING IS AN area of swordsmanship in which very subtle differences separate the novice from the expert. Though there are many other important aspects of the art, an intuitive awareness of distance is crucial for those aspiring to become master swordspersons. The difference in a single foot's position at the outset of an interaction with swords can entirely change the number of steps required to engage an opponent. One inch too far away and you may fail to block an oncoming strike. One centimeter too close and you may get cut.

DISTANCING DRILLS

This section will help you develop a feel for how distance is related to strategic advantage. Practicing simple exercises with *bokken* will accomplish this. Because a purely theoretical understanding is useless when you face a real opponent, these drills are designed to teach you at an intuitive level. After practicing each drill many times, you will find that you can make accurate predictions about the success or failure of an attack simply by taking note of the distance between you and your opponent. You will know instantly whether to step forward before entering or to hold your ground in anticipation of your opponent's movement. You will feel exactly how far you need to reach with your sword to make contact.

Getting to such a high level is not easy, however. When you practice these exercises, remember to adopt the different visual focus levels at the appropriate times. Experiment with each level, and consider how the area you focus upon affects your ability to perform these drills. A narrow focus works best when you are first attempting to coordinate a practice drill with your partner. A broad, all-encompassing focus works best once you have practiced a drill repeatedly and have added speed and power.

Strive to adhere to the fundamentals you learned in the section on sword-handling drills. Consider whether you are holding your sword in a correct, strong position, and whether its position relative to your partner and your partner's sword are strategically sound. Having practiced the previous drills with concentration, you should have a good understanding of how to position both yourself and your sword. Proper sword handling will help you distance yourself correctly, just as attention to distancing will inform your sword handling.

Practice the exercises as often as you can, with as many different training partners as you can, constantly striving to deepen your awareness and understanding of the principles being taught. Your ability to feel the exchange of energy between you and your opponent will emerge only if you dedicate yourself to these drills and strive to increase your awareness whenever you practice. Come back to these drills after you have read the sections on angles, timing, and mastering swordsmanship. These distancing exercises are very effective in developing the advanced states of mind discussed in those sections.

Neutral Distance

For the purposes of this chapter, we will define the neutral, or middle, distance as that which causes an attack (either yours or your opponent's) to miss by a hair's breadth. Maintaining this distance at all times results in neither opponent cutting the other, and neither being cut. You must develop an awareness of this distance so that you can practice safely.

Maintaining a neutral distance allows you to avoid an attack at the moment it occurs and then to immediately close the distance so your counterattack is successful. Closing the distance before an attack allows you to preemptively cut an opponent before she has a chance to cut you. Opening the distance forces your opponent to step or move before being able to reach you, thereby creating extra time and distance within which you can take correct action. You must consider these different distances carefully, practicing constantly so that you instinctively recognize both the distance and its tactical importance.

As always, practice these drills until you can confidently step to the exact appropriate distance, just far enough away to avoid being hit, but not more than an inch away from the tip of your partner's sword. As you get better, add speed and power to the cuts to create a more realistic interaction, but use extreme caution since any strike with a sword or *bokken* can cause serious injury.

EXERCISE 28: HORIZONTAL DRAW AND CUT

For *nukitsuke* (the horizontal draw and cut), stand facing your partner, both of you in kendo stances (right foot flat, left foot slightly back with the heel off the ground, and both knees slightly flexed). Try to estimate how far away you must stand so that your partner's draw will just miss touching you, and move to that distance. Have your partner draw, slowly and carefully, without either of you taking a step (see fig. 45). If your opponent's sword touches you, or if there is more than one inch of space between the tip of her sword and your body, start the drill again, trying to place yourself so that you achieve the minimum safe distance. Repeat this drill until you can confidently step to the correct

Fig. 45. The attacker's nukitsuke *(on the left) should just miss the defender's body.*

opening distance every time. Reverse roles so that you can confidently draw your sword to within an inch of your partner's body.

Face your partner, both of you in kendo stances in the extended ready position with your swords crossed. Have your partner attack, thrusting forward, sliding her front foot forward if necessary, in an attempt to touch your body with the tip of her sword. Your goal is to be far enough away that the thrust just fails to touch you (see fig. 46). However, to make this drill worthwhile, you must attempt to establish this distance when you first cross swords, then maintain your distance when the thrust occurs (rather than moving back as the thrust approaches). If you find that you are too close or too far, completely break contact, reestablish the crossed-sword position, and start the drill again. Be sure to practice both the attacker's role and the defender's role so that you gain an intuitive understanding of this distance from both perspectives.

Fig. 46. The attacker's thrust (on the left) should just miss the defender's body.

EXERCISE 30: DOWNWARD CUT

Face your partner, both of you in long stances in the extended ready position with your swords crossed. Have your partner attack, stepping forward to an upright stance and raising her sword overhead, while you step back, also raising your sword. Your partner will then step forward into a long stance, attempting to touch your body with the tip of her sword while making a downward strike (see fig. 47). You will step backward into a long stance, attempting to move far enough away so that your opponent's strike just misses you. If you find that you are too close or too far, completely break contact, reestablish the crossed-sword position, and start the drill again. Once you become comfortable with your ability to avoid an overhead strike, reverse the roles so that you are the attacker.

Fig. 47. When the attacker (on the left) cuts, the defender steps back just far enough to make the cut miss.

Inside

"Inside" refers to any position from which your opponent could touch you or cut you without taking a step. The inside distance cannot be maintained for long periods of time. Instead, whenever a swordsperson finds himself inside, he must be prepared to parry, attack, or increase the distance from his opponent. The inside position is useful to force a withdrawal, to preemptively stop a draw, or (used in conjunction with angular stepping) to move inside an attack at the moment it occurs.

Practice these drills until you can confidently step to the exact distance desired. Use extreme caution since these drills involve actual contact with the *bokken* and could result in injury. Do not add speed or power to the cuts in these drills regardless of how confident you feel about them.

Stand facing your partner, both of you in kendo stances. Try to estimate how far away you must stand so that the edge of your partner's sword will touch you approximately six inches below its tip as she completes her draw. Move to that distance. Then have your partner draw, slowly and carefully, without either of you taking a step. If your partner's sword fails to touch you or if it touches you at a point less than six inches from its tip, start the drill again, adjusting so you are touched at the exact depth you estimate. Repeat this drill until you can confidently step to the correct distance every time. Reverse roles so that you can assuredly draw your sword to perform a deep cut at the exact depth you predict.

Fig. 48. The attacker's nukitsuke *(on the left) should touch the defender at a depth of six inches.*

Face your partner, both of you in kendo stances in the extended ready position with your swords crossed. Have your attacker slide his front foot forward, attempting to thrust so the sword would penetrate your body to a depth of approximately six inches. When the thrust touches you, tense your abdomen and let the thrust push you backward. If you find that you are too close or too far, completely break contact, and reestablish the crossed-sword position to start the drill again. Be sure to practice both the attacker's role and the defender's role so that you gain an intuitive understanding of the correct distance for an effective thrust as well as how to defend against one.

Fig. 49. The attacker's thrust (on the left) pushes the defender backward.

Face your partner, both of you in long stances in the extended ready position with your swords crossed. Have your partner attack, stepping forward to an upright stance and raising her sword overhead, while you step back, also raising your sword. Your partner then steps forward into a long stance while making a slow, careful, downward strike, attempting to contact your head with her sword, about six inches below its tip. Step backward into a long stance, attempting to move just far enough away that your partner's strike contacts you at the desired depth. If you find that you are too close or too far, completely break contact, and reestablish the crossed-sword position to start the drill again. Once you become comfortable with your ability to predict the exact depth of contact for an overhead strike, reverse the roles and repeat the drill.

Fig. 50. When the attacker (on the left) steps into a long stance and cuts, the defender steps back just far enough so that the cut touchs her at a depth of six inches from the sword's tip.

Outside

"Outside" refers to any position from which your opponent cannot touch you or cut you without taking at least one step forward. An outside distance is safer than a neutral distance or an inside distance because it provides more time to react to an attack. It is useful as a means of gathering visual information about an opponent so you can lure him into a committed attack, or as a means to set up your own withdrawal. However, it also adds time and distance to your own attacking moves.

Practice these drills until you can confidently step to the exact distance desired. Use extreme caution, as these drills involve actual contact with the *bokken* and could result in injury. Do not add speed or power to the cuts in these drills, regardless of how confident you feel about them.

EXERCISE 34: HORIZONTAL DRAW AND CUT

For this *nukitsuke,* stand facing your partner, both of you in kendo stances. Try to estimate how far away you must stand so your partner will have to take a full step forward to touch you approximately six inches below the tip of her sword when completing her draw. Move to that distance. Have your partner draw, slowly and carefully, while step-

Fig. 51. *The attacker (on the right) should be forced to take a full step forward in order to bring her* nukitsuke *into contact with the defender.*

ping forward. If your partner's sword fails to touch you, or if it touches you at a point less than six inches from its tip, start the drill again, trying to step so that you are touched at the exact depth you estimate. Repeat this drill until you can confidently step to the correct distance every time. Reverse roles so that you can assuredly draw your sword and cut while stepping, contacting your opponent at the exact distance you predict.

EXERCISE 35: THRUST

Face your partner. You should both be in kendo stances, with enough distance between you that the tips of your swords, in the extended ready position, are at least six inches apart. Have your partner attack. She should be required to step forward to make her sword penetrate your body to a depth of six inches. When the thrust touches you, tense your abdomen and let the thrust push you backward. If you find that you are too close or too far, completely break contact, and start over from the original position. Be sure to practice both the attacker's role and the defender's role so that you gain an intuitive understanding of the correct distance required (one full step) before executing an effective thrust.

Fig. 52. The attacker (on the right) should be forced to take a full step forward in order to bring her thrust into contact with the defender.

Face your partner, both in long stances, with enough distance between you that the tips of your swords, in the extended ready position, are at least six inches apart. Have your partner attack and then step forward to an upright stance, raising her sword overhead, while you step back, also raising your sword. Your partner then steps forward into a long stance, adjusting her steps to cover enough extra distance so that her sword comes into contact with your head about six inches below its tip as she makes a slow, careful, downward strike. Step backward into a long stance, attempting to move far enough away that your partner's strike contacts you at the desired depth. If you are too close or too far, completely break contact and reestablish the crossed-sword position to start the drill again. Once you become comfortable with your ability to predict the exact depth of contact for an overhead strike, reverse the roles so that you are the attacker, and repeat the drill.

Fig. 53. The attacker (on the right) must step forward, covering enough distance so that, when the defender steps back, the cut touches him six inches from the sword's tip.

Stance Considerations

Your stance, and your opponent's stance, can have an enormous effect on the strategic implications of distancing. A more mobile stance means that you can cover distance more quickly. A deeper stance allows you to deliver a more powerful cut, but compromises your ability to move quickly. The following drills will help you develop an intuitive understanding of the pros and cons of each stance.

You should come away from practicing the various stances with a good understanding of when to use each one. A neutral stance is used only for formal positions such as bowing. An upright stance is used during transitions such as moving from one forward cut to another. A kendo stance is used to move forward or backward quickly to attack and for situations in which more power is needed than an upright stance provides. A long stance is used when it becomes necessary to move forward with power and balance, for strong blocks, and for powerful finishing cuts.

It may be more difficult to close the distance between you and your opponent when you are in a long stance than it would be if you were in a kendo stance. When you attempt to close the gap between you and your opponent, you should be cognizant of which stance you wish to end up in, since the way you get to that position will determine the number and size of steps you take. Your posture will also play a critical role.

EXERCISE 37: NEUTRAL STANCE

In situations that do not involve fighting, most of us stand with our feet more or less even in what we call a "neutral" stance. This is not a good stance for swordsmanship, since it is not conducive to moving forward with power and balance. To understand the relative disadvantage of this stance, try facing your opponent in the extended ready position with your swords crossed. Assume a neutral, even-footed stance, and have your partner assume a long stance (one foot forward, the other two and a half to three feet back). If you are trained in any other martial art, you probably already feel a sense of disadvantage. Offsetting her feet creates an immediate advantage for your partner, who can direct power for-

Fig. 54. One partner assumes a neutral stance (on the left) while the other partner assumes a long stance.

ward or backward without leaning, while you must modify your stance before being able to direct power.

Without stepping, try the various sword-handling drills from the previous section, including extension, deflection, blocking high, pressing down, and breaking contact. Your lack of balance and lack of ability to extend with power while in a neutral stance should quickly become apparent. Practice both attacker's and defender's roles so that you gain a full understanding of how these stances affect the interaction.

EXERCISE 38: UPRIGHT STANCE

In *Eishin-ryu* and other systems of iaido, the stance used for quick stepping, and for the intermediate position between long stances, is called an "upright" stance. In an upright stance, one foot is flat on the floor (usually the right foot), and the other foot is balanced on the ball of the foot, placed next to the midpoint of the flat foot. Both knees are bent. Although not as aggressive as a kendo stance (which is described next), this stance is better for a swordsperson than a neutral stance. It allows for better front-to-back balance, better forward mobility, and better delivery of power in a forward direction. However, you will find that an upright stance does not provide sufficient balance to be maintained throughout an entire sword interaction.

To appreciate the relative advantages and disadvantages of an upright stance, try facing your opponent in the extended ready position with your swords crossed. Assume an upright stance while your partner assumes a long stance.

Again try the sword-handling drills. Your balance and ability to extend with power should feel more substantial than they did in a neutral stance. However, you should also notice that your partner is better able to extend power than you because her feet are offset, and she is better able to control her balance because of her lower center of gravity. Practice both attacker's and defender's roles so that you gain a full understanding of how these stances affect the interaction.

Fig. 55. One partner (on the left) assumes an upright stance while the other partner assumes a long stance.

The stance used in kendo is similar to the upright stance in *Eishin-ryu* iaido, but slightly longer. The kendo stance is used for quick stepping and as a setup stance for driving the front leg forward to add power to cuts. One foot is flat on the floor (usually the right foot), and the other foot is on the ball, placed between six and ten inches behind the flat foot. The legs are straight, but the knees are flexed rather than locked. The kendo stance allows for better front-to-back balance, better forward mobility, and better delivery of power in a forward direction than either a neutral or an upright stance. A kendo stance provides for quick forward and backward movement, allowing a *kendoka* to enter and strike at an opponent quickly. In iaido, however, it is primarily a transition stance. It almost always leads to or sets up a deeper stance at the moment of attack, because the major cut that finishes most iaido forms is designed to be a powerful motion that cleaves an opponent's body in two. The great power required to accomplish such a cut compels us to finish in an extended leg posture such as a long stance. Practice both attacker's and defender's roles so that you gain a full understanding of how these stances affect the interaction.

Fig. 56. The feet are reversed in the kendo stance for clarity in the photo. Normally the right foot is forward.

To test the relative advantages and disadvantages of a kendo stance, try facing your opponent in the extended ready position with your swords crossed. Assume a kendo stance while your partner adopts a long stance, and again try the sword-handling drills. Your balance and ability to extend with power should feel more substantial than they did in either a neutral or an upright stance, though you should notice that your partner still has a relative power advantage. Practice both attacker's and defender's roles so that you gain a full understanding of how these stances affect the interaction.

EXERCISE 40: LONG STANCE

The long stance referred to throughout this section is found in *Eishin-ryu* and most other forms of iaido. It is used as the foundation stance for large, powerful cuts and to move forward with balance and power. In this stance, the front foot is flat on the floor, and the back foot is on the ball, with the heel pushed toward the ground but not touching it, about two and a half to three feet behind the front foot. The front knee is bent and the back knee is locked. The long stance allows for very good front-to-back balance and very good delivery of power in a forward direction. Unlike an upright stance and a kendo stance, however, a long stance is less suitable for quick movement.

Fig. 57. Both partners assume a long stance.

Practice the sword-handling drills with both you and your partner in long stances, facing each other in the extended ready position with your swords crossed. Your balance and ability to extend with power should feel more substantial than they did in either a neutral stance or an upright stance. Practice both attacker's and defender's roles so that you gain a full understanding of how these stances affect the interaction.

EXERCISE 41: POSTURE

For general practice, you should keep your back very straight, your shoulders pulled back and down, your chin pulled back, and your knees slightly bent. You should feel a forward-moving energy in your hips, especially during forward stepping and cuts.

Be careful to avoid putting your shoulders or face forward. Operate on the assumption that your opponent has a sword as long as yours, so any position that shortens the distance between you and your opponent places you at risk of being cut (see fig. 59).

Leaning backward is also risky. You may find that you can clear attacks by leaning back, but this puts your lower body at risk and makes it difficult to move quickly (see fig. 60).

Fig. 58. A good upright stance includes a straight back, slightly flexed knees, and a feeling of forward-moving energy in the hips.

Fig. 59. When the defender (on the left) leans forward, the attacker's sword touches him without any other changes in their positions.

Fig. 60. When the defender (on the left) leans backward, the attacker's sword misses his face but touches his body.

Responding to an Opponent

After you develop an awareness of the distance between yourself and your opponent, you must learn to maintain or control it. Your goal is to develop a deep awareness of distance so your feet automatically maintain the proper distance, freeing your mind to process other aspects of an interaction. You can do this by consistently practicing the drills in this chapter while constantly focusing your awareness on the space between your training partners and yourself.

In time, with sufficient practice, our bodies tell us when an opponent is too close. It is difficult to explain how this feels. I feel a constricting tension or nervousness in the pit of my stomach when the distance is too close for safety. Similarly, if I am too far away from my opponent, I feel anxiety when I consider whether to charge in for an attack. You may define your own feelings differently, but awareness of these body signals can be trained and sharpened only by constant practice and by paying careful attention to your gut. Learn to listen carefully to what your body tells you, and it will guide your actions.

Once you are familiar with these response drills, practice them without any particular stance, the active partner stepping freely forward or backward as he sees fit and the other partner responding appropriately. Practice stepping side to side, circle around each other, and vary the pace until you can comfortably maintain a neutral distance at all times. Note that "comfortably" is a relative term. You may have to stay busy to maintain this distance if your partner is active. If your partner has longer legs than you, you may be forced to take more steps to keep up. Only with consistent long-term practice can you become more efficient to compensate for these difficulties.

EXERCISE 42: NEUTRAL DISTANCE —SWORD SHEATHED

Face your partner with your swords sheathed. Have your partner draw and cut with *nukitsuke*. Adjust the distance between you so the cut just misses you (a neutral distance). Then have your partner re-sheathe his sword and step forward or backward at random. Each time your partner steps forward, respond by stepping backward to maintain a neutral distance. Each time your partner steps backward, step forward. Have your partner perform *nukitsuke* to test the distance between you. Repeat this drill, and alternate which partner takes the active role. Practice this drill using an upright stance, a kendo stance, and a long stance. Practice both attacker's and defender's roles so that you gain a full understanding of how these stances affect the interaction.

Fig. 61. *After both partners have stepped, the attacker (on the left) performs* nukitsuke *to test the distance between them.*

EXERCISE 43: NEUTRAL DISTANCE —SWORD DRAWN

Face your partner in the extended ready position with your swords crossed. Adjust the distance between you so that your swords cross about six inches from their tips (a neutral distance). As in the preceding drill, have your partner step forward or backward at random. Each time your partner steps forward, respond by stepping backward to maintain a neutral distance. Each time your partner steps backward, step forward. Try to keep your swords crossed about six inches from their tips at all times. Repeat this drill, alternating roles. Practice using an upright stance, a kendo stance, and a long stance. Practice both attacker's and defender's roles so that you gain a full understanding of how these stances affect the interaction.

Fig. 62. Both partners maintain a neutral distance with swords crossed while stepping forward and backward.

Gaining an Advantage

The most straightforward way to gain an advantage using distance is to move in. However, simply moving in without considering the pros and cons of your position is not strategically sound. A full understanding of how to gain an advantage with distance requires knowledge of sword positioning, angles, and timing. Thus, each of the following drills includes additional aspects that complement the distance component and satisfy our goal of cutting an opponent while avoiding being cut. To deepen your understanding of distancing, revisit these drills after practicing the angle and timing drills in later chapters.

In this drill, a subtle hand angle allows you to close the distance between you and your partner without being impaled on her sword. Face your partner in the extended ready position with your swords crossed, both you and your partner standing in an upright stance. Without losing the extension in your arms, turn your hands to bring your sword's blade edge to bear against the side of your partner's blade. Continue to extend as you step forward, guiding your partner's sword away from your body and bringing the tip of your sword into contact with your partner's chest or abdomen. When done correctly, this combination of motions should allow you to close the distance between you and your partner, cut your partner, and direct your partner's sword harmlessly past your own body. Once inside, you take away your opponent's ability to cut you with extended cutting actions.

Reverse roles so that your partner is the attacker. Whether you take on the attacker's role or the defender's role, pay careful attention to the distance between you and your partner; the feeling in your shoulders, arms, hands, and *bokken,* and the degree of relaxation or

Fig. 63. The defender (on the left) closes the distance while angling his blade to redirect the attacker's sword.

tension in your abdomen. When you are comfortable with this drill, practice it using a kendo stance and a long stance, and then with your eyes closed.

EXERCISE 45: AVOIDING THE CENTER

Face your partner in the extended ready position with your swords crossed, both you and your partner in long stances, each with your right foot forward. Step forward with your left foot to bring yourself into an upright stance while raising your sword overhead. Step forward again with your right foot, moving on a slight angle toward your partner's left shoulder to avoid her extended sword. As you complete the step, turn your body slightly to bring your right hip and shoulder forward, then cut on a downward angle to your partner's clavicle. When performed properly, this motion should allow you to slip past your opponent's extended sword and cut her. This drill is much more difficult to perform than it appears on paper, so you may have to try it several times, varying the length of your steps and the amount of angle you employ before

Fig. 64. The defender (on the left) steps forward to a long stance, angling slightly to the right to avoid the center, moving into an open long stance and then cutting to the attacker's clavicle.

you can comfortably close the distance without running into your partner's sword.

Be sure to reverse roles so that your partner is the attacker and you are the defender. Pay attention to the distance between you and your partner, the line of her extension, the exact angle required to slip past her sword, and the feeling in the center of your body. When you are comfortable with this drill, practice it using a kendo stance. Also practice with your eyes closed.

EXERCISE 46: ENTERING AGAINST A DOWNWARD CUT

Face your opponent in the extended ready position with your swords crossed, both you and your partner standing in long stances, each with your right foot forward. Both you and your partner step forward with the left foot while raising your swords overhead. Before your partner can strike, step forward with your right foot and carefully cut straight down to the top of your partner's head. To actually charge in the face of

Fig. 65. The defender (on the left) quickly steps forward to a long stance, cutting to the top of the attacker's head.

an attack requires courage and superb timing, so this drill should be practiced many times, while focusing on distance and timing, always using extreme caution to avoid hitting your partner.

Switch roles and have your partner be the attacker. Be mindful of the distance between you and your partner, the subtle clues that tell you when your partner is about to move, and the feeling in the center of your body as you gather yourself to charge. It is not advisable to practice this drill with your eyes closed.

EXERCISE 47: SLIDING IN

Face your opponent in the extended ready position with your swords crossed, both you and your partner in upright stances. Have your partner slide her front foot forward to move into a long stance while thrusting straight ahead with her sword. Maintain your position and turn your hands to bring your sword's blade edge to bear against the side of your partner's blade while extending energy through your arms. Guide your partner's sword away from you, bringing the tip of your sword into contact with her chest or abdomen. This combination of motions allows you to close the distance between you and your partner while you direct her sword harmlessly past your own body.

Fig. 66. The attacker (on the right) steps forward with a thrust, while the defender angles his blade to redirect her sword.

Practice this drill carefully, since the "winner" is not controlling the motion's speed and force. Move slowly, gripping your *bokken* lightly, until you have full control of the drill. When you're ready, reverse roles so that you are the defender and your partner is the attacker. It is not advisable to practice this drill with your eyes closed.

EXERCISE 48: AVOIDING THE CENTER
AGAINST A DOWNWARD CUT

Face your partner in the extended ready position with your swords crossed, both you and your partner in long stances, each with the right foot forward. Have your partner attack, stepping forward with her left foot to move into an upright stance while raising her sword overhead. At the same time, without moving, raise your own sword overhead. Just as your partner steps forward with her right foot and executes a downward strike, step slightly to your right with your right foot and execute your own downward strike while pivoting out of the way with your left foot. As you complete the pivot, turn your body slightly to bring your

Fig. 67. When the attacker (on the right) steps forward into a long stance, cutting straight down, the defender steps to the right and pivots with his left foot, angling slightly to the right to avoid the center and cutting to the attacker's clavicle.

right hip and shoulder forward, and cut on a downward angle to your partner's clavicle.

Reverse roles so that your partner is the defender. For the purposes of this drill, focus on the distance between you and your partner, the line of extension, and the exact angle required to slip past your partner's sword.

EXERCISE 49: CHARGING AGAINST A DOWNWARD CUT

The difference between this drill and the entering drill is subtle. Face your opponent in the extended ready position with your swords crossed, both you and your partner standing in long stances, each with the right foot forward. Have your partner attack, stepping forward with her left foot while raising her sword overhead. Raise your sword without stepping. When your partner forms the intention to step forward and strike, carefully cut straight ahead to thrust the tip of your sword into her face. Be careful! This is very dangerous for the attacker, so practice this drill many times, concentrating on maintaining a safe distance. The attacker must be ready to bend backward in a split second to avoid being

Fig. 68. As the attacker (on the right) forms the intention to step forward and cut, the defender suddenly thrusts the tip of his sword toward the attacker's face.

hit in the face, and you must hold your sword gently, staying aware of the split-second distance and timing changes needed to abort the attack if necessary.

Reverse roles with your partner, so you are the attacker and she is the defender. Be aware of the subtle clues that tell you when your partner is about to move and the feeling in the center of your body as your partner prepares to charge.

Cultivating "Feel" in Distancing

As you get better at sword handling and distancing, you should find that your awareness of your sword's position gradually improves. You should also begin to recognize when angles and distances are safe or dangerous. For the intermediate swordsperson, this knowledge takes the form of "feel," an intuitive awareness of the tactical openings in an interaction. The following exercises are designed to help cultivate that awareness.

EXERCISE 50: LINEAR MOTION

Face your partner in the extended ready position with your swords crossed. Have your partner be the initiator. Whenever your partner steps forward, move backward to maintain the distance between you (see fig. 69). When your partner moves backward, you move forward, always attempting to keep a consistent distance between you. Switch roles, then practice this drill in an upright stance, a kendo stance, and a long stance. When you are comfortable with the drill, practice it with your eyes closed. Occasionally trick your partner by moving your sword with your arms rather than stepping.

Pay particular attention to how your sword feels to determine whether it is stationary relative to your partner's sword or sliding against it. When you and your partner are maintaining contact between your weapons without the distance changing, they are considered to be "touching." When the distance is changing, the swords are "sliding." When you develop a high level of tactile awareness of each sword's relative position, you will be able to respond to changes in an instant, as when your opponent attempts to close the distance between you for an attack. While your eyes may miss a subtle shift in distance, your hands will feel the sliding sensation and you will be able to react quickly.

Face your partner in the extended ready position with your swords crossed. Have your partner be the initiator. Whenever your partner steps forward, backward, sideways, or in a circle around you, respond by stepping backward, forward, sideways, or in a complementary circle to maintain sword contact and a consistent distance between you (see fig. 70). You need not maintain any particular stance during this drill, since it is designed to teach you to maintain sword contact and a consistent distance regardless of the direction in which your partner moves. Switch roles. When you are comfortable with the drill, practice it with your eyes closed.

ANGLES

This section will help you develop an intuitive understanding of how angles can provide a strategic advantage. Think of angles not as only movements to the left and right, but also as upward, downward, forward and backward movements.

As you think about the use of angles in swordsmanship, consider the fact that no angular advantage is present when you and an opponent directly face one another, holding your sword in front of you in the same manner. If one swordsperson moves in, out, or sideways, however, particularly along a tactically sound angular path, he will gain an advantageous position. When the person with the advantage follows up with an appropriately timed cut or counterstrike, he may triumph.

One important reason angles can work to your advantage is that, by moving on an angle, you can simultaneously move out of the way of an attack and change the distance between you and your opponent. For example, if your opponent attempts to cut you with a downward strike, you can avoid the strike by moving forward to your left at a forty-five-degree angle. This motion will not only take you out of the way of the

Fig. 69. When the attacker (on the right) steps forward, the defender steps back to maintain the distance between them, concentrating on whether the swords are touching or sliding.

Fig. 70. Whenever the attacker (on the right) takes a step, the defender responds with a complementary step to maintain contact and correct distancing.

strike, it will move you significantly closer to your opponent where you can counterstrike, achieving your primary goal of cutting an opponent while avoiding being cut. Needless to say, angles can be used effectively only if the swordsperson also understands how to evaluate his opponent's position, handle his sword, establish correct distance, and use the principles of timing (which are presented in the next section).

ANGLE DRILLS

Practice these exercises as often as you can, with as many different training partners as you can, constantly striving to deepen your awareness and your understanding of the principles being taught. Repeated practice of these drills will help you discern strong and weak angles and prevail by executing specific techniques that correspond to the openings presented by your opponent.

As you gain expertise, you will find that more and more of your techniques combine two or more of the elements we have discussed. Eventually you will act in accordance with all the principles of swordsmanship, and, if you face an opponent who is missing even a single element, you will triumph. However, when you face a well trained opponent, success will come not from simply knowing a principle or putting it into practice. Instead, it will come from your mastery of the subtleties of each principle and the relationships between the various techniques. These concepts are easily stated in words, but you can only gain expertise by throwing yourself into practice with all your commitment and passion.

Much more about the highest levels of mastery will be discussed in the last chapter of this book. For now, we will consider some of the applications of angles in swordsmanship, employing three positions: sword sheathed with your hands in a position to draw; swords crossed in the extended ready position; and sword overhead, ready to strike.

Sword Sheathed

When you face an opponent whose sword is sheathed, hands ready to draw, you are faced with a finite number of possible attacks. You know, for example, that no downward cut is coming and that a thrusting attack, though possible, would require one or more preliminary motions to put the sword into position. You can be fairly sure, instead, that the first attack will be one of three possibilities: a horizontal draw and cut, an angular downward cut, or a rising draw and cut.

The position of your opponent's hands will help you further narrow down which of these attacks may be coming. If the sword's edge is facing up, she may be planning an angular downward cut. If she has rotated her sword's edge to an outward position, she is probably considering a horizontal draw and cut. And if she has rotated the sword's edge to a downward position, this greatly increases the likelihood that she is planning a rising draw. You can thus move to the most advantageous position to defend and counter each attack.

Have your opponent stand with her sword sheathed and her hands in the ready position for a *nukitsuke* (see fig. 71). By focusing carefully on her hands, you can determine what sort of draw she is planning.

A position directly in front of or to your opponent's right would get you cut by the horizontal draw. Naturally, you want to avoid such a position. Several positions that would be safer are as follows: (1) on

Fig. 71. The attacker's hands show that she is preparing for a horizontal nukitsuke.

your opponent's left; (2) far enough away that the cut will miss you; (3) below the path of your opponent's cut; and (4) if your timing is very good, so close that you could stop your opponent's draw, either with your hand or with a quick draw and preemptive cut. Practice each of these alternatives to develop your sense of which positions are safe and which are vulnerable when facing an opponent who is about to draw.

EXERCISE 52: MOVING TO THE LEFT

This drill uses a subtle forward angle along with a step to the side. Stand facing your partner, both you and your partner in kendo stances with your swords sheathed. Have your partner make a horizontal draw while stepping into a long stance. Pay close attention to the path of her sword. Notice that there is an area at your partner's left through which the blade does not pass. Your goal is to step forward on a slight outward angle (to your right) and into this safe area. When you practice, pay careful attention to the exact angle required to avoid your partner's cut. Though simple in theory, this is one of the most difficult exercises in this book. Focus deeply on every aspect of the interaction to avoid being cut. Practice

Fig. 72. The attacker (on the right) draws with a nukitsuke *while the defender moves to his right to avoid being cut.*

both attacker's and defender's roles so that you gain a full understanding of how the angle affects the interaction.

EXERCISE 53: MOVING AWAY

This drill involves backward movement. Stand facing your partner, both you and your partner in kendo stances with swords sheathed. Have your partner step into a long stance while making a horizontal draw, and adjust your position so that, if you did not move, about the last six inches of her sword would cut you. Your goal is to step backward, left foot first, and move to safety just as the cut passes by. When you practice, pay attention to the timing required to avoid the horizontal cut. Avoid moving too early, since this would give your attacker time to recognize your tactic and move forward to cut you. Practice both attacker's and defender's roles so that you gain a full understanding of how the angles affect the interaction.

Being able to move out of the way of an attack in this manner is important, but keep in mind that this method of avoidance is purely defensive, and, without other elements, does nothing to advance your tactical position. Later drills will provide more proactive tactical elements.

Fig. 73. The attacker (on the right) draws with a nukitsuke *while the defender moves straight back to avoid being cut.*

This drill uses a downward angle followed by an upward angle. Stand facing your partner, both you and your partner in kendo stances with your swords sheathed. As in the last drill, have your partner make a few horizontal draws while stepping into a long stance. Adjust your position so that, if you did not move, about the last six inches of her sword would cut you. Your goal is to crouch, moving underneath the cut just as it passes by. When practicing this drill, notice the timing required to avoid the horizontal cut. Always avoid moving too early, since this would give your attacker time to recognize your strategy and adjust the direction of her attack. Practice both attacker's and defender's roles so that you gain a full understanding of how the angles affect the interaction.

Be sure to maintain your balance while crouching, since you will need to spring upward from this position to complete your own *nukitsuke*. To complete the tactic, practice rising as you complete your draw and cut. It is challenging to adjust for correct distance and to maintain strength in your cut from this position, so repeated practice is required.

Fig. 74. The attacker (on the right) draws with a nukitsuke *while the defender crouches to avoid being cut.*

This drill employs forward movement. Stand facing your partner, both you and your partner in kendo stances with your swords sheathed. Again have your partner make a few horizontal draws while stepping into a long stance, and adjust your position so that, if you did not move, about the last six inches of her sword would cut you. Your goal is to move in quickly and press against your partner's right arm with your left hand before she is able to draw. Extend your left arm so that it is naturally strong. Pay attention to the timing required to beat your partner's draw without giving your opponent time to react. Practice both attacker's and defender's roles so that you gain a full understanding of how the angles affect the interaction.

This movement, by itself, is purely defensive in nature. Unless you are skilled at empty hand combat, the next drill is a better choice as an actual fighting tactic.

Fig. 75. As the attacker (on the right) attempts to draw with a nukitsuke, the defender enters, defeating the attack by pressing against the drawing arm.

This drill uses forward movement with a counterstrike. Stand facing your partner, both you and your partner in kendo stances with your swords sheathed. As in previous drills, have your partner make a few horizontal draws while stepping into a long stance. Adjust your position so that, if you did not move, about the last six inches of her sword would cut you. Your goal is to quickly draw and cut with a forty-five-degree downward angle to your partner's wrist, preventing her from drawing her sword. The timing required to beat the draw is very quick, and you must be sure that your sword ends in a strong cutting position. If either element is missing, this tactic will fail. For example, if you are quick but your sword ends in a weak position, your cut may be overwhelmed by your opponent's *nukitsuke*. Conversely, if your sword arrives in a strong position, but too late to intersect the path of your opponent's drawing arm, you will get cut. Be sure to practice this drill often.

Fig. 76. The attacker (on the right) attempts to draw with nukitsuke, *but the defender stops the draw with a forty-five-degree downward cut.*

Swords Crossed

The next few drills are designed to teach you how various angles can help you avoid a linear attack and improve your strategic position. By this time, you should automatically be aware of such details as the angle of your sword's edge, the intensity of your opponent's gaze, and the potential danger along the straight attacking path of a thrust or downward strike.

EXERCISE 57: THRUST, PRESSING DOWN

This drill uses both a right-to-left entering angle and a subtle downward angle. From the swords-crossed position, have your partner slide her right foot forward into a long stance while thrusting directly forward with her sword. Just as the attack is about to reach you, slide your right foot forward and to the right, taking you on a forty-five-degree angle toward your right, while you press down against your partner's sword with your own (see fig. 77). You will have to turn your body slightly to the left as you execute this motion in order to maintain a strong position with your hands in front of your body. Repeat this portion of the drill until you develop an intuitive sense of the correct angle and the appropriate pressure to exert on your partner's sword. Switch roles so that you can experience the drill from the attacker's perspective.

Continue by practicing the following, paying careful attention to the interplay of distance and timing as you do so. After having stepped forward on a right angle to avoid your partner's thrust, bring your left foot forward to adopt an upright stance, raising your sword overhead. Have your partner hold her position. Pause a moment to reflect on how the strategic relationship between you and your partner has changed (see fig. 78). Note the closeness and the fact that you are inside her most effective range of attack.

To finish this interaction, consider how far you are from your partner. If you are close, adjust the distance by sliding your left foot backward toward your right rear to assume a long stance, cutting to your partner's right collarbone (see fig. 79). If you can reach your partner without moving, simply cut from where you stand. If you are too far away, slide your right foot forward to adopt a long stance while cutting.

Fig. 77. As the attacker (on the right) steps forward into a long stance and thrusts, the defender steps forward at a forty-five-degree angle to his right while pressing down the attacker's sword.

Fig. 78. After moving inside the attack, the defender (on the left) steps to an upright position and raises his sword.

Fig. 79. The defender (on the left) finishes the interaction by stepping back with his left foot while cutting to the attacker's collarbone area.

If you are too far away to cut your partner's body, cut her arms. Practice this drill, letting the feel of the interaction sink into your bones, experimenting with the many different possible distances between you and your partner.

EXERCISE 58: THRUST, PARRY

This drill uses a forty-five-degree defensive angle to the left, followed by a complementary forty-five-degree angle of counterattack. Face your partner with your swords crossed, both you and your partner in upright stances. Have your partner slide her right foot forward into a long stance while thrusting directly forward with her sword. Just as the attack is about to reach you, slide your left foot forward and to the left, taking you on a forty-five-degree angle toward your left front. Parry by raising your sword with your hands to the left (see fig. 80).

Once you have parried the thrust, raise your sword overhead and pivot by moving your right foot in an arc toward your left rear corner. Turn your body slightly to the right while you strike toward your partner's head (see fig. 81).

Fig. 80. When the attacker (on the right) steps forward into a long stance and thrusts, the defender steps to the left while raising his sword to parry the thrust.

Fig. 81. The attacker (on the right) maintains a thrust position while the defender pivots back with his right foot and counters with a strike to the head.

This is one of the most common avoidance and counterstrike movements in Japanese swordsmanship. Many subtle variations of angle and counterstrike will result in success. Repeat this drill until you intuitively sense the possible angles and timing, and be sure to switch roles so that you can experience the drill from the attacker's perspective.

EXERCISE 59: THRUST, CONTROL WITH EDGE

This drill uses a subtle redirecting angle from right to left. Face your partner with your swords crossed, both you and your partner in upright stances. Have your partner slide her right foot forward into a long stance while thrusting directly forward with her sword. As the thrust comes toward you, turn your blade edge slightly to the left to redirect it. Making this motion correctly requires slightly turning your shoulders to the left, fully extending your arms, and slightly turning your wrists and forearms. Done properly, the redirection will cause the thrust to move harmlessly past you while the tip of your own sword points directly at your partner's midsection.

Fig. 82. As the attacker (on the right) steps forward into a long stance and thrusts, the defender redirects the attack by shifting his sword's edge to the left.

Normally, to finish this motion, you would thrust to your opponent's midsection. However, there are a variety of other choices available to you once you pass inside the effective range of an attack, including a rising cut, a horizontal slash to the abdomen, or a downward strike. After mastering the initial defensive motion, experiment with all the variations on counterstrikes that you know until you determine which work best for you. Practice both attacker's and defender's roles so that you gain a full understanding of how the angles affect the interaction.

Attacker's Sword Overhead

Unlike situations in which your opponent has to raise her sword before striking, when an interaction starts with your opponent's sword in an overhead position, you lose any timing advantage. For example, in the previous sheathed-sword exercises, there is a slight delay before the initial cut as your opponent draws her sword. In the swords-crossed exercises, any attack other than a thrust requires your attacker to move her sword before striking. When her sword is overhead, however, she need only strike downward. There is no interval between initiating the attack and actually attacking, meaning that you will have no time to evaluate, but must respond instantly. Because of the requirement for instant action, you should develop a set of tactical responses to have ready in the event that your opponent moves to an overhead position. These responses include disengaging, redirecting, entering, and attacking.

Disengaging can involve taking a step sideways, backward on an angle, or straight backward, far enough to avoid a strike and into a position that is tactically neutral or advantageous. In redirecting, you use your own sword to deflect an attack. When entering, you step forward to take your body out of the sword's path. Attacking means you either add a counterstrike to an entering motion or aggressively move your sword to a position that prevents the opponent's downward strike.

Working in your favor is the fact that an overhead position provides limited tactical choices for your opponent. Every attack she makes will consist of a downward motion, whether it be a straight downward cut or an angular cut, so her attack is predictable. Moreover, the forward commitment required for a downward cut creates a tactical opening on either side of the cut, allowing you to enter on an angle. Despite the fearsome appearance of an opponent with her sword raised to strike, you can move to a position of safety with relative ease. The key is to ensure that you are in a mobile stance at the moment when your opponent prepares to strike.

EXERCISE 60: DISENGAGING BACKWARD

This drill has you move straight backward to avoid an attack. Face your partner with your swords crossed, both you and your partner in long stances, each with your right foot forward. Have your partner raise her sword to an overhead position while stepping to an upright stance. Do not wait until the strike begins. Instead, immediately step backward into an upright stance. Your partner will strike straight downward while

Fig. 83. Just as the attacker (on the right) steps forward and strikes, the defender steps backward into a long stance, causing the strike to miss.

stepping forward into a long stance. Just as her strike begins, step back into a long stance, allowing the strike to pass harmlessly (see fig. 83). Practice both attacker's and defender's roles so that you gain a full understanding of how the angles affect the interaction.

Keep in mind that this method of avoidance, like some of the earlier ones, is purely defensive. Without other elements, it does nothing to advance your tactical position. Later drills will provide more tactical benefits.

EXERCISE 61: DISENGAGING RIGHT

This drill uses a forty-five-degree right-to-left angle to avoid an attack. Face your partner with your swords crossed, each of you in the extended ready position with your right foot forward. Have your partner raise her sword to an overhead position while stepping into an upright stance. Immediately step to the right with your right foot.

Fig. 84. As the attacker (on the right) steps forward to an upright stance, raising her sword overhead, the defender steps to the right with his right foot.

Fig. 85. Just as the attacker (on the right) steps forward and strikes, the defender pivots to the side with his left foot, causing the strike to miss.

Have your partner strike straight downward while stepping forward into a long stance. Just as the strike begins, pivot to your right rear with your left leg, allowing the strike to pass by harmlessly. Practice both attacker's and defender's roles so that you gain a full understanding of how the angles affect the interaction.

Because this drill is designed to teach you how to move out of the way of attack, no counterstrike is included. However, using elements of earlier drills, you should be able to add suitable blocks, parries, and counterstrikes to make this drill more realistic.

EXERCISE 62: REDIRECTING

This drill uses a subtle right-to-left angle and redirects the attack. Face your partner with your swords crossed. Have your partner raise her sword to an overhead position while stepping forward, and then strike straight downward. Step back into an upright stance and then, just as

Fig. 86. Just as the attacker (on the right) steps forward and strikes, the defender pivots off the line of attack and redirects the strike with his sword.

the strike commences, pivot slightly and use your sword to redirect your partner's sword. As soon as her sword passes your body, carefully thrust toward her face. Practice both attacker's and defender's roles so that you gain a full understanding of how the angles affect the interaction.

EXERCISE 63: ENTERING WITH COUNTERSTRIKE

This drill uses a forty-five-degree left-to-right angle to avoid an attack. Face your partner with your swords crossed. Have your partner raise her sword to an overhead position while stepping forward, and then strike straight downward. Just as the strike begins, step quickly to your left front corner with your left foot. Raise your sword to an overhead position to parry the attack (see fig. 87). Immediately pivot backward and to your left with your right foot to ensure that your body is out of the strike's path. Let your sword swing behind you as you pivot, then counterstrike. Practice both attacker's and defender's roles so that you gain a full understanding of how the angles affect the interaction.

Fig. 87. As the attacker (on the right) begins her downward strike, the defender steps forward to his left with his left foot while parrying the strike.

EXERCISE 64: ENTERING WITH ATTACK

This drill uses a strong right-to-left movement across the plane of the attack. Face your partner with your swords crossed. Have your partner raise her sword to an overhead position while stepping forward, and then strike straight downward. Just as the strike begins, quickly step forward with your left foot to your left front corner. Before the strike is complete, step strongly forward with your right foot to pass your partner on her right side. Let your sword drag along your partner's right side to execute a body cut (see fig. 88). Practice both attacker's and defender's roles so that you gain a full understanding of how the angles affect the interaction.

In summary, these are just a few of the countless movements that you can use to avoid being cut and to set up your counterattack. After practicing these drills, consider other options for how to move, and explore the tactical opportunities that each different movement provides. Be

Fig. 88. Just as the attacker (on the left) completes her downward strike, the defender steps strongly forward with his right foot and cuts the attacker's right side.

sure to practice each movement sufficiently. There are few activities in which it is more dangerous to be mediocre than swordsmanship. Your time is far better served by mastering one or two skills than it is by learning an entire encyclopedia of techniques without truly being able to perform any of them.

TIMING

Timing is a swordsperson's ultimate skill. Every technique described in this book is merely academic unless you can perform it with correct timing. A sword in the correct defensive position that arrives too late will not block an attack. A step made too early, though it may take you to the proper distance, will allow your opponent to adjust his attack to reach you first. Moving at a strategic angle at the wrong time will result in a loss. In real combat, being cut with a Japanese sword, however slightly, carries a high likelihood of death. Thus, it is critical for a swordsperson to act and react at the perfect moment.

It is important to draw a distinction between timing and speed. Speed is not a sword master's primary characteristic. Indeed, as Miyamoto Musashi said, "The long sword cannot be wielded quickly." If we engage in many matches, the chances are good that we will face opponents who are faster than we are. Even those of us who are naturally fast will have days when we feel sluggish. Moreover, as we age, our reflexes will slow. We cannot always rely on being the speediest swordsperson in the dojo. What we can rely on is our trained mind's ability to detect tactical openings whenever they arise, whether before an attack, during an attack, or just after an attack.

The key to good timing is to develop a deep understanding of the principles of swordsmanship so that you move into tactically sound positions at the right instant. This understanding must be accompanied by a relaxed, alert state of mind, allowing you to perceive an opponent's intentions just as he begins to move. Recognizing that internal calm is necessary and working to achieve it in every encounter will help you deepen your skill. The better you are at eliminating extraneous thoughts and quieting your mind, the better you will be at sensing your opponent's intentions. As you practice the timing drills detailed in this section, pay close attention to your state of mind. After you have practiced each drill a few times, work toward adopting the reflective mind discussed in the section on visual acuity drills. Paradoxically, you will feel more energized after an hour of practice than you did before starting. You will prevail in more and more encounters. Your encounters with opponents will become less like tense conflicts and more like refreshing meditation sessions.

Consistent, long-term practice is of paramount importance for good swordsmanship. Study the timing drills that follow. Practice them over and over again. Incorporate elements from earlier lessons, such as correct sword handling, distancing, and the use of angles. Come back to these drills after you have read the final chapter on mastering swordsmanship, and practice them in accordance with the mastery process explained there. Even the simplest drill becomes complex when you are cognizant of all the factors that go into expert swordsmanship. At first, you may find it difficult to coordinate all the factors. If you are persistent, however, the components will come together, you will experience the state of flow that practitioners of the martial arts seek, and you will emerge as an effective swordsperson with a keen, balanced mind.

TIMING DRILLS

These drills require split-second timing, and mistakes are not uncommon. To avoid injuries, I recommend that you use *shinai,* the split bamboo swords made for kendo practice. If you are confident, you may use *bokken,* but please practice with extreme caution to protect yourself and your training partners. In any case, take the time to set up and practice the drills in slow motion before trying them at full speed.

Go no Sen *(Opponent's Initiative)*

For our purposes, the expression *go no sen* will refer to an interaction in which your opponent initiates the attack. Normally, this is considered an inferior timing situation since, all other factors being equal, you will lose when you are the second person to act. The master swordsperson, however, can see the opportunities for defense and counterattack when an attacker commits to a certain attack. The following three exercises will teach you three levels of response to a *go no sen* attack, from least to most desirable.

EXERCISE 65: OPPONENT PREVAILS

Adopt the extended ready position in a kendo stance. Have your partner do the same. Adjust your distance so that your swords cross about six inches from their tips. When the distance is set, both you and your partner should pause and take a deep breath, fully relaxing your bodies while staying mentally alert. When ready, have your partner attack, springing forward and quickly raising her sword to strike you on the top of your left shoulder (see fig. 89). Her goal should be to avoid your sword and move quickly so that her strike is completed before you have time to react. Practice both attacker's and defender's roles so that you gain a full understanding of the timing of the interaction.

Fig. 89. The target for the strike is the top of defender's left shoulder.

EXERCISE 66: BLOCK AND COUNTER

Adopt the extended ready position in a kendo stance. Have your partner do the same. Adjust your distance so that your swords cross about six inches from their tips. When the distance is set, both you and your partner should pause and take a deep breath, fully relaxing your bodies while staying mentally alert. When ready, have your partner attack, springing forward and quickly raising her sword, attempting to tap you on the top of your left shoulder. As soon as you recognize your attacker's intent, raise your sword to block the strike (see fig. 90).

Instantly upon blocking, pivot to your left and swing your sword around to strike to the top of your attacker's head (see fig. 91). Practice both attacker's and defender's roles so that you gain a full understanding of the timing of the interaction.

Fig. 90. The defender (on the left) raises his sword to block.

Fig. 91. Having blocked, the defender (on the left) pivots to the left and counters.

Adopt the extended ready position in a kendo stance. Have your partner do the same. Adjust your distance so that your swords cross about six inches from their tips. When the distance is set, both you and your partner should pause and take a deep breath, fully relaxing your bodies while staying mentally alert. When ready, have your partner attack, springing forward and quickly raising her sword, attempting to tap you on the top of your left shoulder. As soon as you recognize your attacker's intent, move slightly to your right to avoid the strike while quickly countering by tapping your attacker on top of her left shoulder. Done properly, the counterstrike should happen at the exact moment when the original strike would have landed, had it not been avoided. Practice both attacker's and defender's roles so that you gain a full understanding of how the timing affects the interaction.

Fig. 92. Having avoided the strike, the defender (on the left) counters.

Sen no Sen *(Simultaneous Initiative)*

Here, *sen no sen* refers to an interaction in which both partners initiate the action at exactly the same time. This is not an uncommon occurrence for opponents who are evenly matched, but *sen no sen* also happens in bouts where one opponent is more experienced because tactical openings may become available to both participants in the same instant. *Sen no sen* is a fantastic opportunity for a skilled swordsperson who is already in motion when an opponent's attack comes. There are many subtle adjustments that can lead to victory if your perception and skill are up to the task. The following exercises are designed to show three varieties of *sen no sen* interactions, from least to most desirable.

EXERCISE 68: OPPONENT PREVAILS

Adopt the extended ready position in a kendo stance. Have your partner do the same. Adjust your distance so that your swords cross about six inches from their tips. Both partners then step back to upright stances,

Fig. 93. At a prearranged signal, the attacker (on the right) springs forward while raising her sword, attempting to touch the top of the defender's left shoulder. The defender moves at the same time, attempting to touch the top of the attacker's left shoulder.

swords raised overhead. When the distance is set, both you and your partner should pause and take a deep breath, fully relaxing your bodies while staying mentally alert.

Before you begin, arrange some type of signal to coordinate your movements. For example, it could be a verbal count or a swaying back and forth of your bodies. At the signal, have your attacker spring forward, quickly raising her sword and attempting to strike you on the top of your left shoulder. You have the same goal, but, for the purposes of this drill, deliberately move just a bit slower than your attacker, resulting in her strike touching first. Practice both attacker's and defender's roles so that you gain a full understanding of how the timing affects the interaction.

EXERCISE 69: CLASH

Adopt the extended ready position in a kendo stance. Have your partner do the same. Adjust your distance so that your swords cross about six inches from their tips. When the distance is set, both you and your

Fig. 94. Because the partners move at exactly the same speed and have the same targets, their swords clash.

partner should pause and take a deep breath, fully relaxing your bodies while staying mentally alert. Arrange a signal beforehand so that you can coordinate your movements. At the signal, both you and your partner should spring forward, attempting to touch the other partner on top of the head. However, just as the strikes begin to come forward, both you and your partner should move together so your swords come into contact in a vertical position, resulting in a clash (see fig. 94).

In kendo, two partners might attempt to push off from a clash and execute a second strike, with the faster or more skilled partner prevailing. Feel free to try it, although the purpose of this particular drill is simply to acquaint you with how an interaction feels when both partners attack at the same time and move at the same speed. Be careful not to injure your partner.

EXERCISE 70: EVADE AND COUNTER

Adopt the extended ready position in a kendo stance. Have your partner do the same. Adjust your distance so that your swords cross about six inches from their tips. When the distance is set, both you and your part-

Fig. 95. The defender (on the left) moves slightly to his right and turns his shoulders, avoiding the attacker's strike and making contact with his own strike.

ner should pause and take a deep breath, fully relaxing your bodies while staying mentally alert. Arrange a signal beforehand so that you can coordinate your movements. At the signal, both you and your partner should spring forward, with your attacker attempting to enter straight in and touch you on top of your left shoulder. You will evade by moving slightly to your right and turning your shoulders to the left, at the same time striking to your attacker's left shoulder (see fig. 95). Practice both attacker's and defender's roles so that you gain a full understanding of how the timing affects the interaction.

Sen Sen no Sen *(Advance Initiative)*

Sen sen no sen refers to an interaction in which you initiate the attack. Though this seems most desirable, keep in mind the lessons learned in the first two parts of this section. Often, moving first means giving away your intentions. For a good swordsperson, forewarned is definitely forearmed.

The purpose here is to help you become a master swordsperson. To do so, you must develop a feel for every type of interaction and learn to master all of them. Taking the initiative is good policy if you are good enough to keep it. If you are as fast or faster than your opponent, you will prevail. If you are smarter than your opponent, you will prevail. If you can trick your opponent into reckless action, you will prevail. Thus, while *sen sen no sen* has its own potential weaknesses, it is the timing of choice because it maximizes your chances of success. Keep in mind, howwever, that not every movement that starts an interaction with swords is a strike. Many other movements can form the basis for a tactically sound attack. The following exercises are designed to show three varieties of *sen sen no sen* interactions: direct attack, tricking the opponent into attacking when you expect it, and anticipating the opponent's attack.

EXERCISE 71: PREVAIL BY ACTING FIRST

Adopt the extended ready position in a kendo stance. Have your partner do the same. Adjust your distance so that your swords cross about six inches from their tips. When the distance is set, both you and your

Fig. 96. *The attacker (on the right) intentionally moves just a bit slower than the defender so the defender's strike touches first.*

partner should pause and take a deep breath, fully relaxing your bodies while staying mentally alert. As the defender, have your partner spring forward, quickly raising her sword and touching you on the top of your left shoulder. You have the same goal, but, for the purposes of this drill, have her move a bit slower than you, resulting in you touching first. Practice both attacker's and defender's roles so that you gain a full understanding of how the timing affects the interaction.

EXERCISE 72: PREVAIL BY TRICK

Adopt the extended ready position in a kendo stance. Have your partner do the same. Adjust your distance so that your swords cross about six inches from their tips. When the distance is set, both you and your partner should pause and take a deep breath, fully relaxing your bodies while staying mentally alert. As the defender, entice your partner to attack by deliberately breaking contact between the swords. As your attacker springs forward, quickly raising her sword and attempting to touch you on your left shoulder, evade by moving to your right and ex-

Fig. 97. The defender (on the left), being fully aware of the attack's timing, evades by moving to his right.

ecuting a counterattack (see fig. 97). Practice both attacker's and defender's roles so that you gain a full understanding of how the timing affects the interaction.

EXERCISE 73: PREVAIL BY ANTICIPATING AN ATTACK

Prevailing by anticipating an attack is the most challenging timing drill. You may have to practice it many times before you prevail on a regular basis. This drill helps you learn to sense when an opponent is about to attack so you can spring into action first.

Adopt the extended ready position in a kendo stance. Have your partner do the same. Adjust your distance so that your swords cross about six inches from their tips. Step back into upright stances, swords overhead (see fig. 98). When the distance is set, both you and your partner should pause and take a deep breath, fully relaxing your bodies while staying mentally alert. Have your partner form the intention to attack and, if you do not act first, have her follow through, attempting to spring forward and touch your left shoulder with her sword. Do not initiate a counter. Instead, wait until you can sense your attacker's intention to move, whether that sense arises from some motion on your attacker's part, a flicker of her eyes, or simply an unexplainable feeling. As soon as you are sure that the attack is imminent, quickly move in and attempt to touch your attacker's shoulder before she can move. Your attacker has the same goal, but, for the purposes of this drill, will deliberately move a bit slower than you, resulting in you touching first. Practice both attacker's and defender's roles so that you gain a full understanding of how the timing affects the interaction.

Fig. 98. When the defender (on the left) senses that the attack is about to happen, he springs forward, attempting to touch the attacker on top of her left shoulder. The attacker moves at the same time, attempting to touch the top of the defender's left shoulder.

4

OKUDEN
(ADVANCED
CONCEPTS)

READING AN OPPONENT

NOW THAT YOU have begun to acquire an expert swordsperson's skills, you can turn your attention to evaluating your opponent. Indeed, mastery of this art requires that you develop the ability to instantly sense your opponent's strengths, weaknesses, and intentions. In what has by now become a martial arts cliché, Sun Tzu advised, "If you know the enemy and know yourself, you need not fear the result of a hundred battles."

If you have worked diligently to learn the principles taught in this book, half your work is already done. By learning how and where to direct your attention, you have improved your ability to recognize the moment when your opponent's attention falters. By learning how to wield your sword, you have learned when your opponent's sword is weak. Learning correct distancing has taught you to sense when your opponent is too close or too far away. Practicing angular avoidance and counterattack drills has helped you identify opportunities when your opponent moves into a dangerous position. Your understanding of timing should now include the ability to respond to your opponent's timing, whether he is initiating an attack or reacting to yours.

OPPONENT-READING DRILLS

On the simplest level, reading an opponent is nothing more than seeing his positional strengths and weaknesses. If you have thoroughly practiced all the drills leading up to this chapter, it should be a fairly simple matter to look at your opponent's static position and readily evaluate it. The amount of bend in his front knee, the angle of his sword, and his distancing will each help you understand what sort of attack or defense is most likely to succeed.

Still more information can be obtained by watching your opponent move. You can learn about his ability by observing whether his balance is good or bad, whether his sword movements are smooth or jerky, and whether his rhythm is confident, hesitant, purposeful, or vague. For that reason, it is sometimes a tactical necessity to force your opponent to move. As you know by now, you can do this by attacking, offering a target, or retreating.

The deepest aspect of learning to read an opponent is the more difficult one. It involves feeling his intentions so that you can defeat an attack just as it occurs. Such a deep understanding requires you to use all your senses. Your eyes determine the strengths and weaknesses in your opponent's stance, your ears tell you when he inhales or exhales, your nose helps you decide whether he is brave or fearful, and your sword gives you feedback on his tactical readiness. Your mind combines all this information to give you an accurate reading of your opponent's readiness to attack.

Another way to describe this advanced form of observation is to say that you are attempting to feel the flow of energy (*ki* in Japanese, *chi* in Chinese) between you and your opponent. Though some people dislike using such an esoteric concept in the otherwise very precise world of swordsmanship, it can be a useful form of shorthand to describe the proper synergy of all the concrete perceptions discussed above. An experienced swordsperson has trained his eyes, mind, body, and sword. In the world of interacting with swords, it turns out that an expert can perceive, with a high degree of accuracy, an opponent's tactical mood.

To achieve the greatest possible awareness of your opponent's intentions, your state of mind is crucial. A negative state of mind interferes with your ability to read an opponent, while a positive state of mind facilitates energy flow. It may seem odd to say that you should feel a sense of goodwill toward an opponent but, if you are well trained, going into battle with a light heart and a confident feeling is better than wearing armor and a helmet. A highly trained, happy swordsperson is best able to infer an opponent's intent.

Indeed, at the highest levels, success in swordsmanship is directly tied to the quality of one's character. A swordsperson with a strong, healthy, and focused mind will triumph over one with a weak, diseased, or scattered mind in virtually every battle, regardless of how much training the latter has had. By throwing yourself into your training—body, mind, and spirit—you give yourself the chance to experience the very character benefits that put you in a position to prevail. Much more will be said about this in the final section of this book.

EXERCISE 74: THE FOUNDATION DRILL

Face your partner with your swords crossed, both you and your partner in long stances. Have your attacker step forward into an upright stance, raising her sword overhead, then step forward into a long stance while striking straight toward your head. In response, step backward into an upright stance, raising your sword overhead, then step backward into a long stance while defending against your attacker's downward strike with a counterstrike that enters at a slight angle (see fig. 99). On odd-numbered repetitions, counter by bringing your sword in from the right side, and on even-numbered repetitions, counter from the left. Repeat this sequence as many times as necessary to complete the drill, with your attacker moving forward and striking each time, and you moving back and countering. For each of the exercises in this section, we will use the same pattern of stepping and repetitive attacks; add the tactical or attitudinal component described.

Fig. 99. The attacker (on the right) steps forward into a long stance while striking to the defender's head. In response, the defender steps back into a long stance while countering with an angular stroke from his left side.

Tactical Weaknesses

EXERCISE 75: VISUAL FOCUS

In this drill, you enter when your attacker loses her visual focus. Start the foundation drill. Face your partner with your swords crossed, both of you in long stances, each with your right foot forward. Have your attacker step forward into an upright stance, while raising her sword overhead, then step forward into a long stance while striking straight toward your head. In response, step backward into an upright stance, raising your sword overhead, then step backward into a long stance while defending against your attacker's downward strike with a counterstrike that enters at a slight angle.

After one repetition, have your attacker deliberately look away from the interaction while moving in to attack. At the moment when your attacker's attention wanders, quickly shift out of the way of the attack and counterstrike to her head as the attack passes harmlessly by. On a right-side repetition, slide your right foot forward and slightly to the right, then slide your left foot back and slightly to the right as you

Fig. 100. As the attacker (on the right) begins her downward strike, the defender steps back and to the right with his left foot, thereby evading the strike, while countering to the attacker's head.

counter. For a left-side repetition, slide your left foot forward and to the left, then slide your right foot back and slightly to the left. Practice both attacker's and defender's roles so that you gain a full understanding of how the loss of visual focus affects the interaction.

EXERCISE 76: SWORD HANDLING

In this drill, you counter when your attacker fails to keep enough extension in her arms during the attack. Start the foundation drill: Face your partner with your swords crossed, both of you in long stances, each with your right foot forward. Have your attacker step forward into an upright stance, raising her sword overhead, then step forward into a long stance while striking straight toward your head. In response, step backward into an upright stance, while raising your sword overhead, then step backward into a long stance while defending against your attacker's downward strike with a counterstrike that enters at a slight angle.

When you're ready, have your attacker deliberately give up her extension by cutting with her arms held too close to her body. As the faulty strike descends, shift back just enough to avoid being hit. At the

Fig. 101. Detecting the loss of extension, the defender (on the left) steps back just enough to avoid being cut.

moment when the strike safely passes your body, cut with maximum extension, leaning forward from your shoulders to ensure that your cut effectively reaches your attacker's head. Practice both attacker's and defender's roles so that you gain a full understanding of how the lack of extension affects the interaction.

EXERCISE 77: DISTANCING

In this drill, you suddenly enter against an attacker who tends to move too close during an attack. Start the foundation drill: Face your partner with your swords crossed, both of you in long stances, each with your right foot forward. Have your attacker step forward into an upright stance while raising her sword overhead, then step forward into a long stance while striking straight toward your head. In response, step backward into an upright stance, raising your sword overhead, then step backward into a long stance while defending against your attacker's downward strike with a counterstrike that enters at a slight angle.

On each repetition, have your attacker deliberately move aggres-

Fig. 102. To cover more distance, the defender (on the left) steps through an upright stance to an effective range for a thrust.

sively forward, closing the distance, so you are within easy striking distance of one another. After the first repetition, take advantage of your attacker's failure to keep a safe distance by thrusting the tip of your sword at her face. If the distance is very close, you may be able to accomplish this simply by stepping forward into an upright stance as you extend your sword. If you need to cover more distance to make the thrust effective, step into a long stance until you reach an appropriate position to close the distance. Practice both attacker's and defender's roles so that you gain a full understanding of how proximity affects the interaction.

EXERCISE 78: TIMING

In this drill, you enter when your attacker's timing falters. Start the foundation drill: Face your partner with your swords crossed, both of you in long stances, each with your right foot forward. Have your attacker step forward into an upright stance while raising her sword overhead, then step forward into a long stance while striking straight toward your head. In response, step backward into an upright stance, raising your sword overhead, then step backward into a long stance

Fig. 103. Sensing the attacker's hesitation (on the right), the defender quickly moves forward to strike.

while defending against your attacker's downward strike with a counterstrike that enters at a slight angle.

After the first repetition, have your attacker deliberately step first but hesitate momentarily before striking. Use the interval between the step and the strike to begin your counter. Quickly step in and strike (tapping the top of your partner's left forearm) before her strike can begin. Practice both attacker's and defender's roles so that you gain a full understanding of how the disrupted timing affects the interaction.

Attitude

As you consider the following drills, it is important to recognize that they illustrate oversimplified variations in attitude. The drills are useful in getting you to think about how you respond to different types of opponents. However, a single opponent may exhibit different characteristics depending on how an interaction unfolds. An aggressive opponent whose attacks are repeatedly frustrated may become passive. A neutral opponent who discovers some weakness in your swordsmanship may become aggressive in an attempt to defeat you. Moreover, a savvy opponent may display characteristics of one or more of these attitudes in spite of having a different internal state. A nervous opponent may act aggressive to try to cover up fear, or a confident opponent may act passive to invite a reckless attack.

It is up to you to detect the changes in your opponent's attitude and respond accordingly. You must constantly work to deepen your awareness of your opponent's condition so that you recognize his actual state of mind. Start by practicing the drills as they are set forth, then gradually add combinations of attitudes or deceptive attitudes as you become better able to respond to your opponent.

EXERCISE 79: THE AGGRESSIVE OPPONENT

An opponent's aggression can manifest itself in many ways. His rhythm may be quick, his weight may be biased more toward his front leg, his sword may be especially extended during strikes, or his attention may be very narrowly focused. In most cases, he will exhibit several of these characteristics. For practice, ask your partner to fix the idea of being aggressive in his mind by thinking something like, "I am going to attack strongly and conquer my opponent." Practice the foundation drill a few times while your opponent incorporates a faster rhythm, a forward-weighted stance, greater extension, and an intense gaze.

Though more aggressive attacks can be intimidating, after several repetitions you should start to recognize openings. These usually arise because an eager attacker is very committed to and focused on moving forward. If you simply move backward, blocking your opponent's attacks, you will eventually be overwhelmed. However, if you use what you know about angles and timing to avoid the attacks, you should be able to counter successfully. Many techniques can be employed to accomplish this, but one that works well is the Entering with Attack drill we practiced in the previous chapter (see page 105).

Start the foundation drill again, having your attacker adopt aggressive characteristics: Face your partner with your swords crossed, both of you in long stances, each with your right foot forward. Have your attacker step forward into an upright stance while raising her sword overhead, then step forward into a long stance while striking straight toward your head. In response, step backward into an upright stance, raising your sword overhead, then step backward into a long stance

Fig. 104. *Just as the attacker (on the right) begins her downward strike, the defender steps forward with his left foot while bringing his sword to his right side.*

while defending against your attacker's downward strike with a counterstrike that enters at a slight angle.

When initiating a new repetition, just as the strike begins, quickly step forward with your left foot to your left front corner. Before the strike is complete, step strongly forward with your right foot to pass your partner on her right side. Let your sword drag along her right side to execute a body cut as you pass. Practice both attacker's and defender's roles so that you gain a full understanding of how aggression affects the interaction.

EXERCISE 80: THE NEUTRAL OPPONENT

A neutral opponent does just enough to stay even. His rhythm may vary, though he will often attempt to match yours. He tends to keep his weight evenly balanced over both legs. A neutral opponent extends his sword only as much as required to execute a strike, to block, or to redirect your attacks. His gaze will be alert, but without great energy. To practice facing a neutral opponent, ask your partner to fix the idea of neutrality in his mind by thinking something like, "I am going to stay safe and avoid overcommitment." Practice the foundation drill a few times while your partner incorporates a neutral rhythm, an even-weighted stance, a neutral extension, and a relaxed gaze.

You will soon recognize openings that you can take advantage of by varying your rhythm. Because your partner tends to respond to the timing you create, you can set him up to move at a certain pace, then quickly speed up to beat the timing of his next strike. One technique that works well for this is the Prevail by Anticipating an Attack drill we practiced in the previous chapter (see page 117).

Start the foundation drill again, having your attacker adopt neutral characteristics: Face your partner with your swords crossed, both you and your partner in long stances, each with your right foot forward. Have your attacker step forward into an upright stance while raising her sword overhead, then step forward into a long stance while striking straight toward your head. In response, step backward into an upright stance, raising your sword overhead, then step backward into a long

Fig. 105. When the attacker (on the right) steps forward to an upright stance, the defender springs forward, touching the attacker on her left forearm before she can respond.

stance while defending against your attacker's downward strike with a counterstrike that enters at a slight angle.

On the first few repetitions, adopt a relatively slow rhythm, and have your partner try to respond by matching your rhythm. As your attacker forms an intention to attack, quickly move in, raising your sword, and touch your attacker's forearm before she responds (see fig. 105). To keep the exercise authentic, be sure to move quickly enough that your strike touches before your partner's strike is complete. Practice both attacker's and defender's roles so that you gain a full understanding of how neutrality affects the interaction.

EXERCISE 81: THE PASSIVE OPPONENT

Passive opponents actually set themselves up to lose. They do this by waiting to attack until you begin your response, moving slowly when a quick movement is appropriate, keeping their weight on their back legs, or failing to fully extend their arms in cuts or blocks. A passive opponent's gaze will be dull, without energy, and may focus on areas other than those where the action is. To practice facing a passive opponent, ask your partner to fix the idea of passivity in her mind by thinking something like, "I know I am going to lose eventually." Practice the foundation drill a few times while your partner incorporates passive timing for attacks, back-weighted stances, a lack of extension, and a dull gaze.

You will recognize many openings with a passive partner. Because your partner's movements are hesitant and slow, you can defeat her in many ways. One effective technique employs an aggressive follow-up to the initial block.

Start the foundation drill again, having your attacker adopt passive characteristics, especially a slow, hesitant rhythm: Face your partner with your swords crossed, both you and your partner in long stances, each with your right foot forward. Have your attacker step forward into an upright stance while raising her sword overhead, then step forward into a long stance while striking straight toward your head. In response, step backward into an upright stance, raising your sword overhead, then step backward into a long stance while defending against your attacker's downward strike with a counterstrike that enters at a slight angle.

On one of the repetitions, follow up your counterstrike by imme-

Fig. 106. The defender (on the left) dashes the attacker's sword to the side.

diately dashing your partner's sword to the side and stepping in for a finishing stroke. Practice both attacker's and defender's roles so that you gain a full understanding of how passivity affects the interaction.

As you practice this drill, you will learn that a passive swordsperson cannot survive for long. From this you can infer that a knowledgeable swordsperson will not adopt a passive attitude except as a ruse to trick his opponent into attacking. Keep this in mind and proceed cautiously, always striving to sense your opponent's true tactical mood.

Adding Realism

When you are comfortable with the tactical weakness and attitude drills, you can add elements of realism by varying the tactical weakness or attitude presented. Instead of agreeing ahead of time which vulnerability your attacker will display, have him choose randomly. The moment you recognize which one is being presented, execute the appropriate counterattack.

To take a further step toward realism, try varying your counterattack in response to each weakness or attitude you perceive in your partner. While not every counter will be appropriate for every tactical opening, many can be modified to work in more than one situation. Practice applying each technique against all the openings that seem appropriate. Once you have found a set of reliable counters, practice over and over until you are able to instantly apply the right technique at the right moment. It is considerably more difficult to actually do this than it is to write about it, however, so you will likely find that developing skill in this area requires several months of training time.

DEVELOPING STRATAGEMS FOR OPPONENT CONTROL

As we discussed in an earlier chapter, it can be said that there are no advanced techniques, only advanced applications. This section will offer you methods for controlling an opponent by employing applications of the many skills we have already discussed. Most are presented in somewhat general language, encouraging you to think about broad tactical approaches that you can accomplish with a variety of techniques. Your goal is to understand each stratagem's tactical benefit, and then practice the techniques that accomplish each tactical goal.

The stratagems are designed to get you to think like a swordsperson, engaging your mind in the business of predicting and controlling your opponent's actions. One stratagem is not superior to another, but the time and manner in which they are used can create superiority.

Several of the stratagems represent opposite perspectives of similar interactions, reinforcing the idea that your mind is the key to victory. For example, a swordsperson intent on victory may allow his opponent to cut his wrist in order to create an opening for a decisive counterattack. The opponent, however, may be determined to cut several extremities to weaken the first swordsperson before charging in for a finish. The victor will be the one who executes his strategy most successfully.

If you want to be able to predict your opponent's actions (as you certainly must if you aspire to be a great swordsperson), you must study these simple tactics carefully. With your partner, set up each scenario and practice it many times. As you both become more comfortable with a pattern, add speed and intensity. The amount of practice required is monumental, but, if you practice sufficiently, you should develop the reflexive ability to use these methods at will, resulting in a high degree of control over your opponent's actions.

Establish a Pattern

During continuous swordplay, pay careful attention to your opponent's responses to your attacks. If you repeat an attack several times and find that on one occasion your opponent parries without giving it her full energy, follow up with another immediate attack. For example, if you attack toward your partner's right leg several times, each time withdrawing your sword when she blocks, take advantage of your partner's expectations by suddenly attacking her body after she blocks (see fig. 108). The goal is to lull your opponent into a false sense of security by convincing her your attack is not dangerous.

Fig. 107. The defender (on the left) attacks low with a right-to-left strike, causing the attacker to block low.

Fig. 108. The defender (on the left) rides up to cut the attacker's body.

Follow a Direct Attack with an Indirect Attack

Maintain a high level of awareness while interacting with your opponent. Watch for her weak points when you attack. If you find that your opponent fully commits to her defense against a strong attack, recognize that this may cause her to hesitate slightly. Follow up with an indirect attack. For example, if your partner blocks strongly when you strike toward her head, flow suddenly off her block to cut on the opposite side (see figs. 109 and 110).

Set Up Your Opponent

If you want your opponent in a certain position, get her to move into that position by convincing her that it offers some benefit. For example, let your opponent get close every time she thrusts. If she thinks she has almost cut you, she is more likely to thrust again. When you know a follow-up thrust is coming, slip past it and strike to your partner's forehead (see fig. 111).

Fig. 109. The defender (on the left) strikes the attacker's head with a right-to-left angular strike, causing the attacker to block strongly.

Fig. 110. The defender (on the left) pivots his sword around to cut the right side of the attacker's neck.

Fig. 111. When the attacker (on the right) follows up with a thrust toward the defender's midsection, the defender slips the thrust and strikes the attacker's forehead.

Fig. 112. The attacker (on the right) cuts with a downward strike, and the defender suddenly counters.

Invite Attack with Passivity

Typically, a high level of attacking energy will encourage an opponent to defend him or herself. Conversely, as we discussed in "The Passive Opponent," a passive opponent invites attack. Use this principle to invite attack, thereby setting up your opponent. If you maintain awareness, you can read your opponent's position, choice of angles, timing, and pattern, and you can take advantage of this information to create an opportunity to attack. For example, have your partner attack several times while you simply block without attempting to counter. Once a pattern is established in which you demonstrate that you are unlikely to counter, break your pattern and suddenly counterattack (see fig. 112).

Give Up Small Targets to Set Up Big Ones

You can convince your opponents to attack with more and more conviction if you reward them for their efforts. Let your partner hit a few small targets, paying careful attention to her actions, and then enter with a decisive strike when she exposes an opening. For example, if your partner is able to reach in and touch your left wrist, causing you to release your grip on your sword (see fig. 113), she may overcommit with her follow up. This is your opportunity to slip in and counter (see fig. 114).

Use Terrain Favorably

Whenever you find yourself fighting on uneven ground, consider what advantages your position affords you. Rather than limiting yourself to preconceived notions of what constitutes an advantageous position, use your mind to find the advantage. For example, a swordsperson on the high ground has a clear advantage when striking high on her opponent's body (see fig. 115). Lower ground, which normally is considered a disadvantageous position, can create a benefit when attempting to strike using an upward angle (see fig. 116). You will have to work to perceive both a terrain's advantages and disadvantages, however, since a swordsperson on low ground must always be mindful of a committed downward strike from his opponent, and an elevated swordsperson must always guard her legs.

Fig. 113. The defender (on the left) releases with his left hand.

Fig. 114. The defender (on the left) spins his sword and counterstrikes.

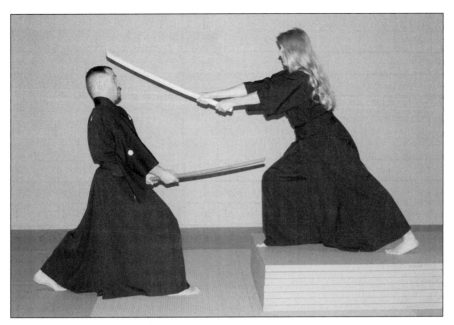

Fig. 115. When the defender (on the right) is on high ground and the attacker is on low ground, the defender can prevail by striking from above.

Fig. 116. When the defender (on the left) is on low ground and the attacker is on high ground, the defender can prevail by employing an upward angle.

Exhaust Your Opponent

You can sometimes prevail by letting your opponent exhaust him or herself. For example, if you find that you can block and parry your opponent's attacks with confidence, allow her to attack continuously until you notice that the tempo of her attacks is slowing. At that point, change the pattern and counterattack.

Fig. 117. When the attacker (on the right), timing, moves her sword back for a third attack, the defender suddenly counters.

Attack Your Opponent's Extremities

Most swordsmanship historians agree that attacking extremities was a crucial part of early sword fighting, perhaps even more important than the full-body cuts we generally finish with today. To gain an advantage, find poorly guarded extremities that you can attack, such as the wrists, knees, or ankles, and continue attacking them until your opponent is so weakened that she offers you an opening for a finishing attack (see fig. 119).

Fig. 118. When the attacker (on the right) strikes, the defender evades and cuts her wrist.

Fig. 119. When the weakened attacker (on the right) releases her sword with one hand, the defender executes a finishing attack.

Fig. 120. While the defender (on the left) waits in a ready position, the suspicious attacker hesitates.

Show Weakness to Engender Suspicion

You can use the appearance of weakness to prevail by creating hesitancy or suspicion in your opponent. If your opponent believes you are a superior swordsperson, show weakness or passivity. This can cause her to hesitate, believing that you are trying to trick her. At the moment of hesitation, strike suddenly (see fig. 120).

MASTERING SWORDSMANSHIP

Mastering swordsmanship is very difficult. Our martial arts backgrounds are as varied as our fingerprints, each of us coming to the dojo with a different degree of talent. The trajectory of our lives does not always maximize our opportunities to become experts. Most students lack sufficient time and discipline to make quick progress. Those who can devote hours to practice, and who have the willpower to do so still face barriers to advancement. Even for the truly gifted swordsperson, one barrier to mastery is the simple fact that he may not have a clear plan for how to proceed. Indeed, forty years of martial arts study has shown me that there is no such thing as a "one size fits all" method for achieving mastery.

However, if you are truly committed to success, there are common steps you can apply both to your technical swordsmanship and to your personal development. Using these steps to guide your training can help you understand what to focus on first, what to look for when you begin to make progress, and where you may be straying from the path of efficient personal development.

Develop Self-Mastery

It should be clear that you can learn nothing profound without a commitment to constant practice and reflection. The advice in this chapter can only be understood in the context of regular training sessions involving strategic interactions between swordspersons. An academic understanding is insufficient. You must internalize each lesson if you wish to advance your swordsmanship and your character.

As in every previous exercise, the keys to true understanding are careful reading, diligent practice, and deep reflection. You must make swordsmanship a part of your daily life. If you do so, you will one day look back and be astonished at how much your abilities and your character have improved.

FOCUS ON THE GOAL

Progress in our swordsmanship requires us to constantly focus on our goals. We aspire to cut our opponent without being cut and to move toward perfection of character. It is critical to remember these aspirations whenever we practice and not to get sidetracked by aspects of training that do not move us forward. This does not mean that we ignore details or fail to practice complicated techniques. On the contrary, a swordsperson's keen awareness should take in every facet of an interaction. Focusing on the goal simply means that we evaluate the various strategic and tactical characteristics of our practice. If something furthers our progress, we continue to practice it. If not, we put it aside.

When facing an opponent, for example, we notice a detail and immediately characterize it in tactical terms. If the angle of our opponent's sword is too acute, we recognize that that allows us to move closer and may provide an opening for attack. Such a detail is important because it may help us prevail. If our opponent happens to wear a purple *hakama,* we may find it amusing, but, because it has no bearing on our tactical approach, we simply file the information away without taking any action.

When choosing a technique, we must carefully consider whether practicing it will be an effective use of our time. After careful reflection, if we find it useless, we discard it. If we can improve it, we modify it accordingly. When we experience a mood or feeling during practice, we consider whether it is helpful to our tactical state of mind. If not, we find a way to cultivate a more beneficial mood.

We make the greatest progress when we are obsessive about our pursuits, constantly focusing on a specific goal. This is true in martial arts, in creative endeavors, or in business. When we are easily sidetracked or frequently change our mind about our goals, we don't accomplish much. On the other hand, if we know exactly what we want and consistently reevaluate our actions to ensure that we are on the right path, we generally reach the highest levels in our field.

To develop character, we strive to become deeper and more in tune with our art, with our opponents, and with the principles of right action. We do this by training with energy and commitment, by reminding ourselves to pay careful attention to the feedback we get from the people and the world around us, by reflecting on our growth to ensure that we are on the right path, and by seeking the advice of those who have gone before us, whether that advice is found in books or in the words of our teachers.

Focusing on the goal means knowing what you want, carefully considering how to get there, consistently evaluating your progress, turning away from dead ends, and choosing the best or most efficient means of moving forward. To advance in Japanese swordsmanship, remember the goals and keep them uppermost in your mind as you set out to learn the techniques.

LEARN THE ESSENTIAL TECHNIQUES

Once you have established your goals, set out to learn the tactics and the techniques that help you move toward them. Practice tactical exercises such as those found in this book. In swordsmanship, the techniques of choice are the formal iaido kata and *kenjutsu* and kendo drills. Study all the legitimate techniques that you can find, whether from a qualified teacher, a book, or a video. As you study, pay careful attention to each component of each technique, making sure that you understand not only how to do them, but also why they are done a certain way and what they are intended to accomplish.

Many new martial arts students try to invent techniques. While their creative spirit is admirable, techniques invented by novices are not usually effective or efficient. Creativity in martial arts, as I explained in *Budo Mind and Body,* is the expression of mastery, not a means of achieving it. Many great martial artists have come before us, perfecting their skills during a lifetime of practice, so it pays to be humble about your own ability to create something new. Follow the rule that greatness follows diligent study of the existing methods. Intuitive leaps are made possible by a deep understanding of fundamental concepts.

To advance in swordsmanship, learn the techniques that constitute your style. Make it a point to learn each one as well as possible, considering your teachers' guidance, the technique's place in the system's overall structure, and how it prepares you to interact with opponents. Determine the exact checkpoints of a properly performed technique, and practice until you can execute all those checkpoints.

MASTER THE TECHNIQUES

After identifying the swordsmanship techniques that help you move toward your goal, master their components by practicing with energy and commitment. Devote yourself to performing each technique as well as you possibly can. Such devotion involves constant practice and frequent reflection on your progress. When you are not practicing, watch others to see if there are aspects of a technique that they are doing better than you. If so, incorporate their methods. If they are making errors, confirm that you are not committing the same ones. Seek out feedback from your teacher, actively requesting advice that will help you improve. Put aside your ego and remember that even the greatest martial artists have room to improve.

The great golfer Tiger Woods is a wonderful example of a person who was able to put aside his ego to improve. After having the most wins of any golfer in the first ten years of his career, he recognized that his swing could be more effective and more consistent. He sought out the advice of the greatest teachers in the game and reinvented his swing. Having done so, he radically improved his game and proceeded to win even more tournaments.

Many of my own most accomplished swordsmanship students are martial artists who had achieved high ranks in arts such as karate, jujitsu, or aikido, yet were able to put aside their advanced knowledge and accept advice from me on how to be better swordspersons. As a result, they have become experts in more than one art. Being able to study swordsmanship like beginners in spite of their other achievements was a critical aspect of their becoming experts.

Indeed, the very act of striving for mastery is one of the cornerstones of our progress toward perfection of character. As we practice our skills over and over, constantly refining them, we begin to get at the essence of martial arts. We become aware of our strengths and weaknesses, building on the former and gradually overcoming the latter. We come to understand exactly how we should perform each technique. We recognize that our negative moods interfere with our ability to perform at our best, and that our positive moods facilitate excellence.

With a great deal of repetition, fatigue overcomes our analytical minds, and the techniques almost begin to perform themselves. At certain magical moments, if all the factors are in place, our bodies flow effortlessly into the correct positions, as if we are watching an interaction rather than participating in it. Small openings in our opponent's defenses seem huge. A fraction of a second contains a hundred perceptions, enabling us to respond instantaneously, and we feel invincible.

Constantly focusing on the goal, we learn the techniques of our art and work tirelessly to master them. Once we achieve mastery of ourselves and our technical skills, we may then turn our attention to our opponents.

Focus on Your Opponent

OBSERVE YOUR OPPONENT

When you are competent in your swordsmanship techniques, begin to pay close attention to your opponent's actions. We have been involved in two-person interactions all along, but your focus during the first stages of development should have been primarily on your own actions: developing the techniques, executing them, and refining them. Now, having achieved sufficient ability that you can act by reflex, you can start to carefully observe your training partners' actions.

We have already discussed much of what you will look for when facing an opponent who is armed with a sword. The issues are the same as those you encountered while improving your own tactical skills, such as whether your opponent wields his sword in an effective manner, whether he stands too far away or too close, and whether he uses angles and timing effectively. In the dojo, you can repeatedly interact with an opponent and thereby learn a great deal about how he behaves. In each interaction, focus your attention on one aspect and analyze it carefully before considering another element.

For example, watch the way your opponent moves forward to engage you. Is he balanced when moving forward, with an appropriate posture that suits the drill's purpose? Are his feet positioned to give him the best possible means of moving forward to attack? Does he properly synchronize the motions of his sword with the motions of his body?

At this point, discipline yourself to observe carefully without trying to create tactical advantages. Designate a period in your training when you allow yourself to soak up information without attempting to triumph every time. Think of this form of observation as "listening" with your eyes. The more you quiet your inner voice and your will to win, the more your mind will be open to receiving information from each interaction. In The Big Picture, (see page 29) we discussed drills meant to help you develop a reflective mindset. Recall your state of mind as you practiced those drills, and try to reproduce it as you improve your ability to observe your opponents.

The skills you develop during this type of training will benefit you in all areas of your life. You are probably already aware that most people in Western countries are poor listeners. The few who are good listeners are usually surrounded by friends, since a good listener is highly prized. Many successful people have excelled because they have developed the ability to listen, and as a result they notice things that others miss.

Careful observation is a cornerstone of our continued character development. Hearing what the universe is telling you requires a quiet mind trained to pay attention to subtle cues. Teaching yourself to carefully observe your training partners' actions will help you develop the mindset needed to receive obscure messages. As you improve your observation skills, you can begin to adapt your techniques to respond to your opponent, moving you closer to your goals.

RESPOND TO YOUR OPPONENT

Every response you make to an opponent's attack must be carefully tailored to fit the exact nature of his movements. A tall opponent's sword will move toward you at a different angle than that of a short opponent, and an opponent who is naturally quick will force you to respond more rapidly than one who is slow. You have already mastered your techniques and developed a sharp sense of observation, and now is the time to concentrate on honing your ability to respond based on what you observe. As your responses become more precise, your ratio of success in achieving your primary physical goal—cutting an opponent while avoiding being cut—will improve greatly.

Careful observation will tell you what to expect from each opponent, and you will learn to shape your responses even as attacks unfold. For example, if you notice that your opponent sometimes keeps his weight on his back leg when he attacks, you can formulate a tactical approach that takes advantage of that weight bias. Stay sensitive to the motions leading up to the attacks. When you sense that his weight is primarily on his back leg, match his downward strike, and press downward with your sword while you enter. You may be able to drive him backward with your body to set up a finishing strike. The same tactic might not succeed with an opponent who places most of his weight on a front leg, however. Observations of this sort can mean the difference between victory and loss.

Internal development is part and parcel of this stage of the mastery process. The sensitivity you are developing toward opponents can and should be applied to your experiences outside the dojo. There is constant feedback from your environment, whether you are in a match with swords, at a job interview, or on a walk in the woods. How clearly you receive the messages around you and how accurately you respond to them, keeping your ultimate goals in mind, will determine how successful you are throughout your life. In time, this mindset will permeate your entire existence.

MASTER YOUR OPPONENT

Mastering an opponent means clearly discerning his intent, responding accurately to his attacks, responding at just the right moment, and responding in such a way as to set up a decisive counterattack. This requires competence in all the areas that precede this one, including a keen sense of observation, a strategy that focuses on the goal, and an ability to execute swordsmanship techniques with a high degree of skill.

Learning to master opponents requires consistent, long-term practice. You must have repeated opportunities to observe how your actions affect your opponent and to adjust according to what you observe. There are many formal swordsmanship techniques, and the variations and interplay between opponents in a duel with swords is infinite. Countless practice sessions are required to experience a wide array of attacks and defenses. To truly respond well and dominate your opponent, you must cultivate an unbroken awareness of all the important aspects of each interaction. Like most other factors required for mastery, this one requires constant dedication to the principle of trying to cut an opponent while avoiding being cut. Look for every chance to attack. If you maintain this mindset whenever you practice, your swordsmanship will become increasingly successful.

Your determination can mean the difference between becoming a capable swordsperson and becoming a really exceptional one. After following the progression of skill development drills set forth in this book, you may have found that you can defend against an opponent's attacks without necessarily trying to dominate. Perhaps you occasionally attack without much hope of success. Some students reach a plateau at this level, able to compete with opponents of many skill levels while enjoying themselves, noticing details, and gradually deepening their ability to feel the energy flow between partners. Though they continue to make progress, these students will not become truly masterful until they take it upon themselves to make an effort to dominate every opponent.

You must learn how to dominate in an interaction, even if your personality is not a dominant one. A complete technique in martial arts —whether it be a finishing stroke with a sword, a knockout punch, or a full-point judo throw—requires a unification of technique and intention that is impossible to simulate. Despite the great benefits of solo practice, as in iaido or karate kata, nothing can substitute for the insights and abilities gained by overcoming an opponent who is trying to avoid or overcome your techniques.

Focus on the Interaction

FLOW WITH THE INTERACTION

Faced with an opponent who is armed with a sword and trying to defeat you, you must perform with a strongly wielded sword, at the proper distance and angle, and with perfect timing. In prearranged drills or cooperative practice, you may make a conscious decision to execute a finishing technique. In sparring, however, a technique that originates out of conscious thought will rarely succeed. The interval between seeing an opening and executing a technique is too short to allow for reflection. Instead, a technique must simply "happen" at the instant when the conditions are right. This is possible when you are extremely well practiced in your art and can move without interference from your analytical mind.

To become a master swordsperson, you have to let your highly trained reflexes take over. Though your mind is fully conscious of the interactions between yourself and your opponent, it should not focus on them. Instead, it should stay detached from the swordplay. Do not choose which techniques to use; instead allow your techniques to simply occur by themselves. Your mind should not stop on any single aspect of the battle, but smoothly reflects every detail. This dispassionate, continuous mindset is sometimes called a state of "flow."

It can be very difficult to move from conscious execution of techniques to a state of flow. Even the best practitioners have difficulty overcoming the impulse to control every stroke of the sword. You must have a systematic method for cultivating the proper state of mind.

In theory, the method is simple. Gradually add more and more inputs until your conscious mind is overwhelmed and your trained reflexes take over. You can do this by agreeing ahead of time with your training partner to maintain a feeling of lightness (rather than strength) in your practice, and gradually add speed. Your conscious mind may refuse to let go and deliberately select which techniques to use. Be persistent, however, and engage your partner again and again. If you keep trying, eventually you will be able to suspend conscious thought, and your techniques will begin to "happen" in real time. Over repeated practice sessions, your techniques will also become more effective, particularly as you start to work on the next two stages of mastery: reflecting on the interaction and mastering the interaction.

REFLECT ON THE INTERACTION

When you are able to regularly achieve a state of flow during practice, you can begin to elevate the level of your responses. When a practice session ends, reflect on what took place. What worked well, and what did not? Was there an aspect of a formal technique that interfered with its execution against an active opponent? If you are experienced in martial arts, it should be no surprise to you that some techniques work well in practice but do not work well for sparring. There are many reasons for this; for example, you may not have achieved a high enough skill level or you may need to modify a technique to fit the circumstances of a sparring session.

If your skill level is not as high as you would like it to be, the obvious solution is to continue practicing in a controlled setting until you are ready to try the technique in sparring again. For techniques that you need to modify for use in sparring, determine exactly what you need to change. Make the changes and practice until the modifications are reflexive, then try the techniques again in sparring to determine how well they work.

Do not be discouraged if new techniques seem awkward when you first begin sparring. It is normal to have difficulty achieving a state of flow with new techniques. The key, of course, is to keep practicing, gradually increasing the speed and complexity of your interactions until your conscious mind is overwhelmed and you find yourself acting without analytical thought.

MASTER THE INTERACTION

By now you have experienced the state of flow in at least some of your sword interactions. You have also stepped away from them, thought about how to effectively interact with opponents, and determined how to readily achieve a state of flow. Now is the time to work on mastering each interaction. This means controlling the tenor of an entire battle: the speed, the rhythm, the ebb and flow of energy, and the amount of aggression you put forth. To achieve this extraordinary level of control requires excellence in all the skills already presented, including expertise in technique, a deep understanding of your opponents' actions, an ability to react instantaneously, and an ability to observe and analyze an interaction even as you participate in it.

Constantly observe the give-and-take between yourself and your partners. In the midst of continuous swordplay, you must make conscious decisions about how you want the interactions to develop. How will you prevail? Will you be energetic or passive? Will you accelerate the tempo to overwhelm your opponent? If so, what tactics will you use? What subtle adjustments can you make to bring the character of the interaction in line with your wishes?

Keep in mind, however, that regardless of how accomplished you may be, your aspirations for an interaction with an opponent must be realistic. Unless your ability level is substantially higher than your opponent's, his will to win will also affect the outcome. If you overlook his ability and energy, you will fail. Go into each interaction seeking an acute understanding of your opponent's strengths and tactical approach. If you do so, your chances of success are high.

Begin by selecting drills that offer a chance to interact with your opponent for more than a few seconds. Warm up by running through the drills several times. When you are comfortable with all the elements of the drills, repeat them while concentrating on executing your techniques precisely according to the dictates of your style. Next, modify them to fit your opponent's particular style. Spend a few more repetitions concentrating on your opponent's techniques, analyzing his strengths and weaknesses, adapting to his overall pattern, and trying to perceive his tactical energy.

Now speed up the drills. Pay attention to the ebb and flow of energy between you and your opponent. Notice when you feel dominant and when your opponent is dominant. When you perceive a pattern or a key aspect of the interaction that affects the flow of energy, apply everything you have learned to consciously affect a change. If you want the interplay to be slower, slow it down. If you want to dominate for a larger percentage of the interaction, do so. If you want your opponent to attack more forcefully, lure him into doing so.

Practice making adjustments in the midst of a session without losing your unbroken awareness and sense of removal, your state of flow. When you achieve this, you will be able to direct a battle without stopping to consciously execute the techniques. You will be able to decide what you want to take place, and it will simply "happen" at the appropriate time. This is an extraordinary feeling, and one that is not easily experienced. You can experience it, however, by tirelessly practicing with the goals in mind.

Focus on the Larger Picture

INCREASE YOUR AWARENESS

The first step in focusing on the larger picture is to increase your awareness of your environment while you are engaged with an opponent. What you pay attention to is of little importance at first, since you are simply trying to train your sense of awareness. Begin by choosing a sight, sound, or smell, and pay attention to it while practicing the drills. For example, if there is a fan in the room during the summer months, try to hear the sound of the fan blowing. Or, when your eyes follow your opponent's movements, try to notice the shape of the room behind him. Smell the oil on your partner's *bokken* as it passes your face. Feel the weight of your *montsuki* (kimono) on your shoulders as you move your arms to strike. While working to add this information to your consciousness, be sure that you are maintaining good sword-handling principles, preserving the proper distance, moving at effective angles, and maintaining a tactically sound pattern.

Paying attention to outside factors may take you out of your state of flow. At first, some students cannot continue to spar while focusing on additional stimuli. Some can exchange strikes and blocks with their opponents, but cannot maintain an attitude of domination. You can overcome these hurdles with practice. The point is to keep working until you lose neither your unbroken awareness nor your strategic edge. It may take months or even years to achieve this added level of awareness, but with persistence you will get there.

It can be useful to add a third person to your practice. Ask one of your training partners to provide a distraction. This could be a distinctive movement or a few words. Whatever form it takes, it should be something unexpected. Maintain your strategic attitude while paying attention to the third person's actions. If your swordsmanship unravels, repeat the drill with a new distraction. When you succeed in getting through your drills without losing focus, describe the distraction to the third person. Be as accurate and detailed as possible. The third person will let you know how well you did.

As you improve, increase the demands on your awareness by trying to perceive additional factors around you. The more skilled you become, the more you will become fully aware of your environment. If you struggle with this, go back to a level at which you consistently succeed, then gradually increase your inputs. With sufficient practice, very little will escape your notice. What starts out as a means of making you an invincible swordsperson can eventually bring about remarkable changes in your ability to notice and respond to things in all aspects of your life.

INCORPORATE OUTSIDE FACTORS

Now that you have tuned your senses to detect outside factors in the midst of swordplay, you can begin to incorporate those factors into your strategy. Factors that could have an important effect on the outcome of your contest include people, sounds, light or darkness, obstructions, and uneven or slippery surfaces. For example, a person not directly involved in the interaction might distract your opponent, accidentally interfere with his movements, or join the contest on behalf of you or your partner. Sudden noises could startle or distract your opponent. Bright light or the sudden absence of light could interfere with your opponent's vision. An obstruction could be used to trip your opponent, deflect his strike, or provide you with protection. You can use walls to corner your opponent. Uneven or slippery ground could cause your opponent to stumble. The possibilities for using your environment strategically are infinite, but only if you are aware of such critical factors and can use them to your advantage.

Training yourself to incorporate outside factors involves several steps: (1) prearranged practice, (2) practice with a cooperative partner, (3) basic free practice, and (4) free practice incorporating a state of flow. For prearranged practice, choose an obstruction or distraction in advance. Agree with your partner as to how the interaction will progress. For example, if you choose to use an obstruction to interfere with your opponent's movements, agree in advance that your partner will retreat toward the obstruction as you attack. When he is close to the obstruction, employ a tactic that causes him to stumble over it. Practice using a variety of obstacles, thinking deeply about how to use each one, and experiment until you are comfortable employing many outside factors in your training.

You can also practice with a cooperative partner without telling your partner in advance what outside factors you will employ. Agree in advance that your partner will react defensively, protecting himself from your strikes and moving according to your attacks: backward if you attack aggressively, to the left if you drive him in that direction, quickly if you move quickly, and so forth. Practice moving your partner into position so your obstruction or distraction does its work. This will develop your skill at moving opponents around, and it will also improve your ability to notice and employ outside factors as part of your tactics.

For the basic level of free practice, choose an environment that has several obstructions or other factors you can use tactically. Without planning ahead of time which factors you will employ, engage your partner in lengthy interactions. Consciously employ the various obstructions to disrupt your partner's swordplay. Repeat the exercises until you are completely comfortable using aspects of your environment as part of your strategy.

The ultimate practice method for the material presented in this section is free practice incorporating a state of flow. Using all the skills you have developed to this point, engage your partner in a training area that has obstructions or distractions. Practice until you experience a state of flow. Continue to practice until you can block, attack, advance, retreat, force your partner to move, and employ obstructions, all without allowing your mind to focus specifically on any single aspect of your interaction.

As we discussed previously, while in a state of flow you should be fully conscious of the interactions between yourself and your opponent, but your mind should not focus on them. It should remain separate from the swordplay. Rather than selecting techniques, techniques should simply "happen." Your consciousness should not stop on any single aspect of the battle, instead smoothly reflecting every aspect of your environment and incorporating it in the struggle.

MASTER VICTORY WITHOUT FIGHTING

You will recall that the ultimate aspiration of practice in Japanese swordsmanship is expressed in the phrase *saya no uchi no kachi*. Achieving victory with your sword still in its scabbard is an extraordinary challenge, but you are now close to possessing all the necessary skills to do so. Reflecting on the information presented in these chapters, you will see that you have all the tools in place to completely master an opponent.

You have mastered the techniques of your swordsmanship style. You have taught yourself to pay close attention to your opponent's actions and attitudes and to dominate through the use of superior technique. You have freed your conscious mind from the need to control each technique, and have thereby achieved a state wherein you can adapt to any circumstance without hesitation. Your awareness has increased to take in virtually every detail of your environment during an interaction. To prevail without fighting, you must put into practice everything you have learned. Use your heightened senses to take the right action at the moment a battle begins.

The supreme warrior can prevail the moment he or she enters an arena of battle. For example, suppose that by turning to the left as you enter a courtyard, you place the sun at your back and a pillar at your right side. Your opponent, having expected you to walk straight in, has unwisely hidden to the left of the entrance. He will be unable to attack effectively with the sun in his eyes and the pillar between you. He will realize the futility of attacking an opponent with such keen powers of anticipation. Guided by your heightened powers of observation, you will have acted in such a way that victory is inevitable.

Getting to the appropriate state of mind to win without fighting requires preparation. Most of us do not live in a state wherein our consciousness is fully attuned to our environment, so we must prepare ourselves. Clear away every extraneous thought, fully relax your muscles, and enter a state of flow. Engage your partner and act in accordance with the principles of right action.

Reflect on Enlightenment Principles

It requires a great humility to act in perfect accord with universal principles. We must set aside our selfish or untrained thoughts in order to know what is truly right for a situation. What you must do is not always what you want to do or think you should do. Instead, you must do what is absolutely correct for that moment. The better you have trained yourself, the more closely your objectives will be aligned with right action. The more you are able to perceive the truth in your situation, the more efficient your reflexive actions will be.

RELEASE ALL THOUGHT OF SELF

A swordsperson who has expanded her awareness through tireless practice and self-reflection realizes that the most efficient path to victory does not involve conflict. This realization is of monumental importance because it can free the swordsperson from the need to fight. It is not yet the highest expression of mastery, however, since it is still rooted in the self-interested search for victory. To take the final steps in the path toward character perfection, we must begin by giving up our focus on ourselves.

This may seem to contradict earlier chapters in which I stated that a swordsperson must seek to dominate an opponent. There is no contradiction, however, because the different outlooks come at different times in a swordsperson's career. The first approach is meant for an intermediate swordsperson. To learn the skills and attitudes of swordsmanship, we must zealously practice overcoming others; there is no substitute for the unification of mind, body, and spirit brought about by striving for victory. The second approach is meant for the very advanced swordsperson. To surpass the limitations of technique and become an enlightened person, one must give up the wish to overcome others. A person on the martial artist's path must experience the first stage before being ready to embrace the second.

Selflessness is important to your ultimate development because any reserve of self-interest will prevent you from acting in accord with universal principles. The desire to protect yourself or to enhance your self-image through victory can result in your choosing a course of action that satisfies your ego rather than the one that is most efficient. If your self-image is out of proportion with your abilities, you may become overconfident. You may hesitate if you attempt to protect yourself from harm instead of making the most effective cut.

A selfless swordsperson, on the other hand, will not be overconfident because she is not driven by ego. She will choose an efficient action over a self-aggrandizing one. She will not hesitate, but will act decisively, correctly, and in exact proportion to the circumstances.

True selflessness is not something that can be learned in a short time. You must make swordsmanship an integral part of your life. You must practice daily so that clashing with swords is as normal to you as eating or taking a shower. You must devote yourself to mastering the techniques, interacting with opponents, giving up conscious control of your fighting skills, and becoming aware of every aspect of your environment during an interaction. You must visit the dojo at every opportunity, interacting with other swordspersons again and again, throwing yourself into your art, and giving absolutely no preference to victory or defeat.

After doing this, if all the factors are in place and if you are very lucky, you will experience moments of complete involvement in your swordplay such that no thought of yourself occurs. This state may last for seconds or for hours and then be gone for weeks before returning. As soon as you focus on your practice, thinking "I want more selflessness!" this state will be gone. Strive only for more time to practice your swordsmanship, greater awareness of your surroundings, and a better understanding of universal principles. Continue to train with passion. Reflect on your progress when you do not have a sword in your hands. If you learn to regularly achieve a state of "no self" in your training, you will achieve greatness as a swordsperson.

Just as self-interest creates barriers to swordsmanship's ultimate stages of character development, so does clinging to the idea that you must overcome an opponent. To advance still further, you must give up the notion that there is an opponent to overcome and instead learn to see the situation as it truly exists. At the highest level, there is no "self" and no "other," just a set of circumstances that call for right action.

Like self-interest, fixating on the idea of overcoming an opponent will prevent you from acting in accord with universal principles. You will end up focusing on the person rather than on the entire set of circumstances in an interaction. If you underestimate your opponent's abilities, you may become overconfident. If you overestimate them, you may become fearful.

If you give up your attachment to the idea that there is an opponent to overcome, however, you will be free to objectively evaluate a conflict. You will be neither overconfident nor fearful. You will choose the correct response rather than one motivated by a desire to differentiate yourself from or prevail over your opponent.

Advanced aikido practitioners will understand the benefit of giving up the idea that an opponent must be overcome. When an attacker grabs an untrained person's wrist, that person usually reacts by tensing his muscles and trying to escape using force. An aikidoist, on the other hand, is trained to react with just enough force to resolve the conflict, employing principles of circularity to disarm his attacker without injury. The goal is not to prevail over an opponent, but to bring the situation to a harmonious resolution.

Expert swordsmanship is not much different from this. The natural tendency to clash with attackers limits our growth as martial artists. An overabundant sense of self-preservation makes it difficult to understand other people's points of view. Thinking of others as different, foreign, or as obstacles to be overcome can cause us to behave with excessive hostility. Recognizing the innate harmony in interactions between people, on the other hand, helps us to overcome conflict. If we consider ourselves and other people as equally valuable parts of a universal whole, conflict tends to vanish. In the parlance of contemporary self-help manuals, it is better to seek a win-win outcome than to try to defeat other swordspersons. With this outlook, you will rarely be forced to draw your sword, and you will naturally turn toward peaceful solutions.

LIVE IN ACCORDANCE WITH
UNIVERSAL PRINCIPLES

There are countless obstacles to ultimate success in swordsmanship. The desire for money, status, comfort, and expertise are constant distractions, thwarting our ability to live fully in the moment. When training, if we desire victory too fervently, we invite conflict. If we win contests early in our career, there is a good chance we will mistake the good feelings associated with victory for success in spiritual matters. If we are unable to overcome others in spite of our efforts to adhere to the principles of swordsmanship, we may mistakenly believe that we are on the wrong path. None of these states of being is acceptable to the expert swordsperson.

The beauty of a strategic approach to swordsmanship is that the very act of training helps us overcome obstacles to enlightenment. The techniques are grounded in martial realism, giving us concrete feedback on what works and what does not. If you use angles and timing correctly, you will be able to cut your opponent without being cut. If you fail to properly block a downward strike, you will get cut. If you notice an obstacle and your opponent does not, you will defeat him. Our success is linked to our ability to detect the truth and conform to its requirements. When we judge correctly, we prevail.

The progression of training drills in strategic swordsmanship also moves us closer to character perfection. Each time we add another component to our training, we increase our sensitivity. When the many discrete inputs become too numerous to focus on individually, our analytical mind is overloaded and we are forced to evaluate our tactical situation by feel. We learn to make intuitive judgments about very complex events and, because we have trained ourselves to act in accordance with those judgments, we take immediate right action. The greatest warriors live in a state of harmony with their environment, perceiving the most efficient path and taking the steps to succeed long before the need to draw swords arises. They are great because they have overcome the limiting concepts of self and other and the focus on victory.

Such a state is the swordsperson's ultimate goal. As you have no doubt noticed, it is also a desirable state of mind for life outside the dojo. You can achieve it using the methods described in this book. Being able to take in every detail of your surroundings and then respond in a highly effective manner is useful everywhere. Give up your attachment to notions of self and other, gain and loss, victory and defeat. If you fixate on these ideas, your swordsmanship will suffer. Live fully in the moment and your swordsmanship will be without equal. The Way is in training! There is no more meaningful nor more rewarding pursuit.

INDEX

BOOKS BY NICKLAUS SUINO

The Art of Japanese Swordsmanship

This comprehensive manual on the history, evolution, and practice of Eishin-Ryu (Pure Faith) iaido is illustrated with step-by-step drawings to help students, from beginners to advanced, hone their forms and techniques.

Budo Mind and Body

Budo is about learning more than how to fight; true budo is a way of seeking and uncovering meaning in life. Here, Suino reveals the essential components of budo training, including how to determine the principles behind techniques; how to develop physical strength, technical strength; and strength of character; and how to discipline your mind to really focus and be in the present moment.

Practice Drills for Japanese Swordsmanship

A practical, illustrated workbook that offers *bokuto* (wooden sword) drills to supplement the formal class activity of forms practice. Both single and two-person drills are presented, some common to iaido and kenjutsu, others extracted from iaido forms by Suino and used to teach his own students the proper ways of drawing, parrying, and cutting.